W9-AFH-459

Never Knit Your Man a Sweater*

*unless you've got the ring

Never Knit Your Man a Sweater*

*unless you've got the ring!

22 Handsome Projects for Every Level of Commitment

Judith Durant

Storey Publishing

The mission of Storey Publishing is to serve our customers by publishing practical information that encourages personal independence in harmony with the environment.

Edited by Elaine Cissi and Gwen Steege
Technical editing by Lorinda Gayle
Art direction by Mary Velgos
Cover and text design by Mary Velgos
Text production by Mary Velgos
Cover and interior photographs ©Adam Mastoon
Illustrations ©Alison Kolesar

Text © 2006 by Judith Durant

All rights reserved. No part of this book may be reproduced without written permission from the publisher, except by a reviewer who may quote brief passages or reproduce illustrations in a review with appropriate credits; nor may any part of this book be reproduced, stored in a retrieval system, or transmitted in any form or by any means — electronic, mechanical, photocopying, recording, or other — without written permission from the publisher.

The information in this book is true and complete to the best of our knowledge. All recommendations are made without guarantee on the part of the author or Storey Publishing. The author and publisher disclaim any liability in connection with the use of this information. For additional information please contact Storey Publishing, 210 MASS MoCA Way, North Adams, MA 01247.

Storey books are available for special premium and promotional uses and for customized editions. For further information, please call 1-800-793-9396.

Printed in Hong Kong by Elegance
10 9 8 7 6 5 4 3 2 1

Library of Congress Cataloging-in-Publication Data

Durant, Judith, 1955–
    Never knit your man a sweater unless you've got the ring / Judith Durant.
        p. cm.
    Includes index.
    ISBN 13: 978-1-58017-646-0; ISBN 10: 1-58017-646-1 (pbk. : alk. paper)
    1. Knitting—Patterns. I. Title.

TT820.D765 2007
746.43'20432—dc22

                                                                2006027400

For Philippe,
the only boyfriend I ever knitted for

Contents

67

61

117

101

39

73

43

149

79

Introduction

ARE YOU ONE OF MILLIONS of people who have recently picked up needles and yarn for the first time? Welcome to the ranks of the millions who have knitted before you. Many of you are young and hip and are probably dating. Or maybe you're not so young or not so hip . . . but are still dating.

Young or old, new or seasoned, all knitters have the same natural instincts: You want to make warm and comfy things for those you love. What better way to show you care for your flame than by knitting love into every stitch of a new sweater? But heads up to all of you: Not all boyfriends will appreciate the time you put into hand-knitted garments, and not all boyfriends deserve it. So before you spend one hundred or more hours on a labor of love, you'll need to make sure that it is, indeed, love. There are many steps along the way to love, and *Never Knit Your Man a Sweater* (*Unless You've Got the Ring*) will help you choose a knitting project appropriate to the relationship with your current squeeze.

For example, if you've had three dates with the man of your dreams, do not, under any circumstances, start knitting him a sweater. He could be long gone before you've finished the ribbing. In fact, after three dates, don't even think about knitting something that requires shaping of any sort. Start with a scarf. There are three styles here: a simple knit-and-purl-stitch scarf that looks like a work of art, a stockinette stitch scarf with stripes that will look great in his favorite football team's colors, and a patterned scarf knitted in a cashmere blend that not only is handsome on both sides, but also feels divine.

If you're headed for a long-term relationship, congratulations! You may now progress to some simple, shaped projects. Here you'll find hats, socks, and mittens that are relatively quick to complete so that just in case you were wrong about your relationship, you won't have wasted too much time.

Only when you're very sure your man is "the One" should you begin knitting body-sized garments. Even then, start with a vest; sleeves can add weeks to a project. Once you and your boyfriend are mutually committed, knit away to your heart's content. Included are three sweaters that are sure to please.

With *Never Knit Your Man a Sweater*, you'll find the right project for your guy, and you'll also learn tips and techniques that you can incorporate into all your knitting.

A Note about Yarn and Gauge

I chose yarns that I know and love, but although a particular brand of yarn has been specified for each project, you may choose from other possibilities. Textured patterns and colorwork will usually result in a different gauge from the stockinette stitch gauge serving as the basis for the yarn-band recommendation. I also sometimes use yarn on a smaller needle and at a tighter gauge than that specified for the yarn band in order to get the right fabric drape for a particular project. So in addition to the actual gauge in a pattern, with the yarn specifications, I've included a "yarn band gauge." This should make it easier for you to choose a substitute if the specified yarn is not readily available.

[Check Him Out] Coasters

YOU MET HIM. YOU LIKE HIM. You think he likes you. You want to knit for him. For several reasons, consider knitting these coasters as a first project for your new boyfriend. First of all, you can make a set of four in an afternoon. Next, he should be impressed not only that you knit, but also that you've knitted something for him. If he's neither impressed nor flattered, you've learned a valuable nonknitting tidbit that may deserve consideration!

YARN
Reynolds Saucy, 100% mercerized cotton, 185 yd (169 m)/100 g
Yarn band gauge: 5 stitches and 6.5 rows = 1" (2.5 cm) in stockinette stitch on US 7 (4.5 mm) needles
Color A: 736 Taupe, 1 skein
Color B: 899 Black, 1 skein
Yarn amounts are sufficient to make approximately 10 coasters, depending on how you distribute the colors.

FINISHED SIZE
4" x 4" (10 cm x 10 cm)

GAUGE
8 stitches = 2" (5 cm) in Pattern Stitch (Garter Stitch)
Note: Yarn is used doubled throughout.

NEEDLES
US 10 (6 mm) *or size you need to obtain the correct gauge*

NOTIONS
Tapestry needle

ABBREVIATIONS
CA = Color A
CB = Color B

pattern stitch

Garter Stitch

Knit all stitches every row.

Plain Coasters

Make one solid taupe (CA), one solid black (CB), one checkered using CA and CB, and one with a strand each of CA and CB held together.

SET UP Using two strands of yarn, cast on 16 stitches.

Work in Garter Stitch until piece measures 4" (10 cm). Bind off. Weave in ends with tapestry needle.

Changing Colors

When changing colors, it's important to cross the new yarn with the old yarn to prevent unsightly holes from developing in your knitting, and this may be a little tricky with Garter Stitch. When knitting a right-side row, bring the new yarn (light) *under* then *over* the old yarn (dark) and then make the stitch (fig. 1).

When knitting a wrong-side row, bring the old yarn (light) to the front and bring the new yarn (dark) *over* the old yarn and to the back, then make the stitch (fig. 2).

Checkered Coaster

SET UP With two strands of CA, cast on 8 stitches. With two strands of CB, cast on 8 stitches. Crossing the yarns at each color change to avoid leaving a hole (see Changing Colors, page 14), work as follows:

ROW 1 K8 CB, K8 CA.

ROW 2 K8 CA, K8 CB.

Repeat Rows 1 and 2 until piece measures 2" (5 cm), ending with Row 2. Cut yarn, leaving 6" (15 cm) tails.

ROW 3 Joining new yarns on first row, K8 CA, K8 CB.

ROW 4 K8 CB, K8 CA.

Repeat Rows 3 and 4 until piece measures 4" (10 cm) from beginning.

Bind off all stitches with their matching color. Weave in ends with tapestry needle.

Double Up

If you're using balls of yarn that can be worked from the inside, the easiest way to work with two strands is to pull from the inside and the outside of the ball at the same time. If the ball can be worked from the outside only, wind off half and work from two balls.

[The Burger and a Movie] Scarf

AFTER A FEW SUCCESSFUL BUT LOW-KEY DATES with your new guy, this is the scarf to knit. It looks absolutely fabulous and the uninformed will think the maker is nothing less than a knitting deity.

Of course, all knitting takes time, but this yarn does a lot of the work for you. Noro Big Kureyon is one of the best variegated yarns on the market. The color choices are fabulous and the blending is sublime. The textured check pattern of simple knit and purl stitches is easy to commit to memory, and at four stitches to the inch, the piece works up quickly.

YARN
Noro Big Kureyon, 100% wool,
    175 yd (160 m)/100 g
Yarn band gauge: 10 stitches
    and 12 rows = 4" (10 cm) in
    stockinette stitch on US 8
    (5 mm) or US 9 (5.5 mm)
    needles
Color: No. 4, 2 skeins

FINISHED SIZE
Approximately 9" x 62"
    (23 cm x 157 cm)

GAUGE
16 stitches = 4" (10 cm) in Pattern
    Stitch (Simple Block Stitch)

NEEDLES
US 9 (5.5 mm) *or size you need
    to obtain the correct gauge*

NOTIONS
Tapestry needle

Knitting the Scarf

NOTE The first and last 6 rows, as well as 4 stitches at each end of the needle, are worked in Garter Stitch.

SET UP Cast on 36 stitches.

ROWS 1–6 Knit.

ROW 7 K4, work Row 1 of Simple Block Stitch to last 4 stitches, K4.

ROW 8 K4, work Row 2 of Simple Block Stitch to last 4 stitches, K4.

NEXT ROWS Continue in Simple Block Stitch, working first 4 and last 4 stitches of every row in Garter Stitch (knit every row) until piece measures approximately 61" (155 cm) from beginning, ending with Row 6 or Row 12 of Simple Block Stitch.

NEXT 6 ROWS Knit.

Bind off loosely. Weave in ends with tapestry needle, wash, and block.

---

pattern stitch

Simple Block Stitch

(Multiple of 8 Stitches Plus 4)

ROW 1 *K4, P4; repeat from *, ending K4.

ROW 2 *P4, K4; repeat from *, ending P4.

ROWS 3 AND 5 Repeat Row 1.

ROWS 4 AND 6 Repeat Row 2.

ROW 7 *P4, K4; repeat from *, ending P4.

ROW 8 *K4, P4; repeat from *, ending K4.

ROWS 9 AND 11 Repeat Row 7.

ROWS 10 AND 12 Repeat Row 8.

When Flat Is Good

Use a simple scarf like this one to experiment with different stitch patterns. Just be sure to knit a Garter Stitch border at the beginning, end, and all the way up the sides to produce a flat scarf with tidy edges.

[Dinner Date]
Scarf WITH STRIPES

SO YOU'VE SEEN THIS GUY A FEW TIMES and he's sprung for a night out at a real restaurant. By now you know some of his likes and whether or not he's a sports fan. If he is, this scarf is ripe for knitting in team colors. (This version would fairly represent the New England Patriots, Buffalo Bills, New York Giants, or Houston Texans.) It can also be knit in alma mater colors. Or just knit it in any ol' colors you think he'll like! This project is not a quickie, but it requires minimal concentration once you get going, allowing you to cruise along in meditation mode.

The scarf is knit in Stockinette Stitch horizontally on a long circular needle. It will take some time to get from one end of a row to the other, but each row requires only that you knit it or purl it. Begin with a Provisional Cast-On (see Techniques, page 176) and join the long edges with a Three-Needle Bind-Off (see Techniques, page 177).

YARN
Brown Sheep Company Nature Spun Sport, 100% wool, approximately 184 yd (168 m)/50 g
Yarn band gauge: 6 stitches = 1" (2.5 cm) in stockinette stitch on US 5 (3.75 mm) needles
Color A: N04 Blue Knight, 4 skeins
Color B: N46 Red Fox, 2 skeins
Color C: 730 Natural, 1 skein

FINISHED SIZE
Approximately 7.75" x 70" (20 cm x 178 cm)

GAUGE
24 stitches = 4" (10 cm) in Pattern Stitch (Stockinette Stitch)

NEEDLES
Two 32" (80 cm) circular needles, US 5 (3.75 mm), *or size you need to obtain the correct gauge,* one spare needle (double-pointed or straight) for bind-off, same size

NOTIONS
Tapestry needle, crochet hook, scrap yarn, stitch markers

ABBREVIATIONS
CA = Color A
CB = Color B
CC = Color C

pattern stitch

Stockinette Stitch

ROW 1 (RIGHT SIDE) Knit.

ROW 2 (WRONG SIDE) Purl.

Repeat Rows 1 and 2 for pattern.

Knitting the Scarf

SET UP Using Provisional Cast-On (see Techniques, page 176) and CA, cast on 420 stitches. (Place a marker every 40 stitches so you have less counting to do when checking your total.) Work Stockinette Stitch until piece measures 2.5" (6.5 cm) from beginning, ending with a right-side row.

NEXT ROW (WRONG SIDE) Knit. This creates a turning ridge for the fold line.

NEXT ROWS Beginning with a right-side row, continue in Stockinette Stitch for another 2.5" (6.5 cm), ending with a wrong-side row.

NOTE On this first half of the scarf, change colors at the beginning of right-side rows. When changing colors, leave 12" (30 cm) tails to be used for sewing together the ends.

NEXT ROWS Change to CB and work Stockinette Stitch for 1.25" (3 cm), ending with a wrong-side row.

NEXT 4 ROWS Change to CC and work 4 rows.

NEXT ROWS Change to CB and work 1.25" (3 cm), ending with a wrong-side row.

NEXT ROWS Change to CA and work 2.5" (6.5 cm), ending with a right-side row.

NEXT ROW (WRONG SIDE) Knit. This creates a turning ridge for the other fold line.

NEXT ROWS Beginning with a right-side row, continue in Stockinette Stitch for another 2.5" (6.5 cm), ending with a right-side row.

NOTE On this second half of the scarf, change colors at the beginning of wrong-side rows. This leaves tails on both ends of the scarf for sewing.

NEXT ROWS Change to CB and work Stockinette Stitch for 1.25" (3 cm), ending with a right-side row.

NEXT 4 ROWS Change to CC and work 4 rows.

NEXT ROWS Change to CB and work 1.25" (3 cm), ending with a right-side row.

Finishing

Remove Provisional Cast-On and place stitches on needle. With right side facing you and CB in front, bind off with Three-Needle Bind-Off (see Techniques, page 177).

Use tails to invisibly sew scarf ends closed. Weave in ends with tapestry needle, wash or steam, then block.

[He Made Me Dinner (and It Was Good)]
DIAMOND Scarf

THINGS ARE HEATING UP, both on and off the stove. He invited you to his place for dinner and not only was it edible, but it was also delicious. Good cooking skills are a definite asset, so if it looks like this man's a keeper, go ahead and put the money and effort into this very special scarf. It would look great with his topcoat, but, of course, may be worn as desired.

   The scarf is knitted in a super-soft merino and cashmere blend using a reversible pattern, so it doesn't matter how he puts it on. The knitted pattern has a natural tendency to pleat, which results in a neat and comfortable drape. The border is Seed Stitch, which may draw up slightly tighter than the Reversible Diamond Stitch as you knit, but this will be corrected with blocking.

YARN
Lana Grossa Pashmina, 22% cashmere, 78% merino extrafine, 136 yd (125 m)/50 g
Yarn band gauge: 20 stitches and 26 rows = 4" (10 cm) in stockinette stitch on US 7 (4.5 mm) or US 8 (5 mm) needles
Color: 10 Maroon, 4 skeins

FINISHED SIZE
Approximately 12" x 46" (30.5 cm x 117 cm)

GAUGE
22 stitches = 4" (10 cm) in Pattern Stitch (Seed Stitch)

NEEDLES
US 5 (3.75 mm) *or size you need to obtain the correct gauge*

NOTIONS
Tapestry needle

pattern
stitch

Reversible Diamond Stitch

(Multiple of 15 Stitches)

ROW 1 (RIGHT SIDE) *K1, P13, K1; repeat from * to end of row.

ROW 2 *P2, K11, P2; repeat from * to end of row.

ROW 3 *K3, P9, K3; repeat from * to end of row.

ROW 4 *P4, K7, P4; repeat from * to end of row.

ROW 5 *K5, P5, K5; repeat from * to end of row.

ROW 6 *P6, K3, P6; repeat from * to end of row.

ROW 7 *K7, P1, K7; repeat from * to end of row.

ROW 8 Repeat Row 6.

ROW 9 Repeat Row 5.

ROW 10 Repeat Row 4.

ROW 11 Repeat Row 3.

ROW 12 Repeat Row 2.

Repeat Rows 1–12 for pattern.

pattern
stitch

Seed Stitch

(Even Number of Stitches)

ROW 1 *K1, P1; repeat from *.

ROW 2 *P1, K1; repeat from *.

Repeat Rows 1 and 2 for pattern.

Knitting the Scarf

SET UP Cast on 72 stitches.

ROWS 1–8 Work Seed Stitch.

ROWS 9–20 Work first 6 stitches in Seed Stitch, work center 60 stitches in Reversible Diamond Stitch, work last 6 stitches in Seed Stitch.

NEXT ROWS Continue as established, keeping first 6 and last 6 stitches in Seed Stitch and center 60 stitches in Reversible Diamond Stitch throughout until piece measures approximately 45" (114 cm) from beginning, ending with Row 1 or Row 7 of pattern.

NEXT ROWS Work 8 rows in Seed Stitch.

Finishing

Bind off. Weave in ends with tapestry needle, wash or steam, then block.

[Looking Good]
Laptop Cover

YOUR RELATIONSHIP IS STILL IN THE EARLY STAGES, but are you tired of knitting scarves? Here's a little something that your new beau can carry around and show off to his friends and colleagues.

Knitted in a springy merino, the Slip Stitch Pattern produces a thick fabric that acts almost like bubble wrap. Slide a laptop in the pouch, button it up, and toss it into a backpack with no worry that it will be scratched or damaged. If you have time, consider making a mini pouch for the power cord, using the instructions included here.

YARN
Karabella Yarns Aurora 8, 100% extrafine merino wool,
   approximately 98 yd (90 m)/50 g
Yarn band gauge: 18 stitches and 26 rows = 4" (10 cm)
   in stockinette stitch on US 7 or US 8 (4.5 or 5 mm) needles
Color: 22 Gray, 5 balls for laptop cover and 1 ball for power-
   cord pouch (optional)

FINISHED SIZE
9" x 12.75" (23 x 32.5 cm), stretches to fit a Macintosh 15" (38 cm) Powerbook

GAUGE
16 stitches = 4" (10 cm) in Pattern Stitch (Slip Stitch Pattern)
   Note: Yarn is used doubled throughout.

NEEDLES
US 11 (8 mm) *or size you need to obtain the correct gauge*

NOTIONS
Tapestry needle, one 1" (2.5 cm) button for laptop cover, one
   0.5" (1.25 cm) button for power-cord pouch (optional), sewing needle and
   coordinating thread

ABBREVIATIONS
ssk = slip one stitch, slip one stitch, knit the two stitches together through
   their back loops
wyib = with yarn in back. Take yarn to the wrong side (back) so the carried
   yarn doesn't show on the front side of the fabric.
wyif = with yarn in front. On a wrong-side row, take yarn to the front so the
   carried yarn doesn't show on the front of the fabric.

Slip Stitch Pattern

(Multiple of 4 Stitches Plus 3)

ROW 1 (RIGHT SIDE) *K3, slip 1 wyib; repeat from * to end of row, ending K3.

ROW 2 *K3, slip 1 wyif; repeat from * to end of row, ending K3.

ROW 3 K1, *slip 1 wyib, K3; repeat from * to last 2 stitches, ending slip 1 wyib, K1.

ROW 4 K1, *slip 1 wyif, K3; repeat from * to last 2 stitches, ending slip 1 wyif, K1.

Repeat Rows 1–4 for pattern.

Knitting the Laptop Cover

SET UP Cast on 51 stitches.

ROWS 1–4 Work Rows 1–4 of Slip Stitch Pattern.

NEXT ROWS Continue in established pattern until piece measures 21" (53.5 cm) from beginning.

Decreasing for Flap

ROW 1 Ssk, continue in established Slip Stitch Pattern to last 2 stitches, K2tog. You have just decreased 2 stitches.

ROWS 2–18 Repeat Row 1. *You now have* 15 stitches.

Making the Buttonhole

ROW 1 Ssk, work 4 stitches in Slip Stitch Pattern, bind off center 3 stitches for buttonhole, work 4 stitches in Slip Stitch Pattern, K2tog.

ROW 2 Ssk, work 3 stitches in Slip Stitch Pattern, cast on 3 stitches over the bound-off stitches to complete buttonhole, work 3 stitches in Slip Stitch Pattern, K2tog. *You now have* 11 stitches.

NEXT ROWS Continue decreasing in established pattern until 3 stitches remain. Bind off all stitches.

Finishing

With right side facing out, fold front over back so pouch measures 9" (23 cm) from bottom fold. Sew side seams. To keep upper corners of laptop protected, sew top edge of front (cast-on edge of piece) to back with short seams that are 1" (2.5 cm) from each side.

Weave in ends with tapestry needle. Reinforce buttonhole by working Buttonhole Stitch around it (see Techniques, page 179) using a single strand of yarn and tapestry needle. Fold down flap closure and, using sewing needle and thread, sew button on front to line up with buttonhole.

Knitting the Power Cord Pouch

SET UP Cast on 19 stitches.

ROWS 1–4 Work Rows 1–4 of Slip Stitch Pattern.

NEXT ROWS Continue in established pattern until piece measures 8" (20.5 cm) from beginning.

Decrease for flap as for laptop cover until 9 stitches remain.

Making the Buttonhole

ROW 1 Ssk, work 2 stitches in Slip Stitch Pattern, bind off 1 stitch for buttonhole, work 2 stitches in Slip Stitch Pattern, K2tog.

ROW 2 Ssk, work 1 stitch in Slip Stitch Pattern, cast on 1 stitch over bound-off stitch, work 1 stitch in Pattern Stitch, K2tog. *You now have* 5 stitches.

NEXT ROWS Work 1 more decrease row. *You now have* 3 stitches. Bind off all stitches.

Finishing

With right side facing out, fold front over back so pouch measures 3.5" (9 cm) from bottom fold. Sew side seams. To ensure that contents stay in pouch, sew top edge of front (cast-on edge of piece) to back with short seams that are 0.5" (1.25 cm) from each side. Weave in ends with tapestry needle. Reinforce buttonhole as for laptop cover. Sew button on front to line up with buttonhole as for laptop cover.

[Music to My Ears] iPod Cover

HERE'S ANOTHER ACCESSORY that you can knit for your new boyfriend. The small, sheathlike iPod Nano cover will keep his Nano scratch-free as it moves around in his pocket or backpack. Although knitted in very fine cotton on tiny needles, it's so small that it won't take much time to whip up.

The cover is worked in a very elastic K2/P2 Rib Stitch. In fact, one size could fit both the Nano and the smaller iPod Shuffle, but instructions are provided for each.

YARN

J&P Coats Royale Classic Crochet
Thread Size 10, 100% mercerized
cotton 350 yd (320 m)/ball (ball
weight and knitting gauge not
available)

Color A = 492 Burgundy, 1 ball

Color B = 12 Black, 1 ball

Note: If making solid-color covers,
1 ball is sufficient to make either
cover.

FINISHED SIZES

1.25" x 4.25" for Nano cover and 1"
x 3.75" for Shuffle cover (3 cm
x 11 cm and 2.5 cm x 9.5 cm),
unstretched

GAUGE

Approximately 18 stitches = 1"
(2.5 cm) in Pattern Stitch
(Rib Stitch), unstretched

NEEDLES

Set of four US 0 (2 mm) double-
pointed needles

NOTIONS

Tapestry needle, stitch marker

ABBREVIATIONS

CA = Color A

CB = Color B

---

pattern stitch

Rib Stitch

(Multiple of 4 Stitches, Worked in the Round)

ROUND 1 *K2, P2;
repeat from * to
end of round.

Repeat Round 1
for pattern.

Knitting the iPod Cover

	48 sts for Nano	36 sts for Shuffle
SET UP With CA (CB for Shuffle), cast on	48 sts for Nano	36 sts for Shuffle
Divide stitches evenly onto 3 needles,	16 sts each	12 sts each
Join into a round (see Joining into a Round, page 37), being careful not to twist stitches.		
NEXT ROUNDS Work K2/P2 Rib Stitch until piece measures .75" (2 cm). Change to	CB	CA
NEXT ROUNDS Continue in Rib Stitch until piece measures	4.25" (11 cm)	3.75" (9.5 cm)

Bind off all stitches.

Finishing

Lay flat and sew bottom seam across bind-off edge. Weave in ends with
a tapestry needle.

[Keep His Head Warm]
Watch Cap

WHEN YOUR RELATIONSHIP HAS REACHED THE NEXT LEVEL and you're ready to go to the next level of knitting with a shaped garment, start here with this simple watch cap. It's about as basic as it gets, and a quick knitter can finish this cap in a day.

Made in standard worsted-weight wool using a Pattern Stitch that's a 1/1 Rib Stitch, this cap is very elastic and one size really should fit all. If your boyfriend has a particularly large head, add four or eight stitches.

YARN
Patons Classic Merino Wool, 100% pure new wool, approximately 223 yd (204 m)/100 g
Yarn band gauge: 20 stitches = 4" (10 cm) on US 7 (4.5 mm) needles
Color: 249 Stone Marl, 1 skein

FINISHED SIZE
Approximately 17" (43 cm) around, unstretched, and 10.5" (26.5 cm) deep before folding up cuff; will stretch to up to 24" (61 cm) around

GAUGE
3 stitches = 2" (5 cm) in Pattern Stitch (1/1 Rib Stitch), unstretched

NEEDLES
Set of five US 7 (4.5 mm) double-pointed needles *or size you need to obtain the correct gauge*
Note: You may also use a 16" (40 cm) US 7 (4.5 mm) circular needle until you get to the decrease rounds.

NOTIONS
Tapestry needle

ABBREVIATIONS
ssk = slip one stitch, slip one stitch, knit the two stitches together through their back loops

┌───┐
│ **1/1 Rib Stitch**   **pattern**   │
│   **stitch**   │
│   │
│ ROUND 1 *K1, P1; repeat from * to end of round. │
│   │
│ Repeat Round 1 for pattern.   │
└───┘

Knitting the Cap

SET UP Cast on 112 stitches. Place 28 stitches on each of four needles. Join into a round (see Joining into a Round, page 37), being careful not to twist stitches.

Work in 1/1 Rib Stitch for 8" (20.5 cm).

Decreasing for the Crown

ROUND 1 *Ssk, work pattern as established to last 2 stitches on needle, K2tog; repeat from * to end of round. You have just decreased 8 stitches.

ROUND 2 *K1, work pattern as established to last stitch on needle, K1; repeat from * to end of round.

ROUNDS 3–14 Repeat Rounds 1 and 2 six more times. *You now have* 56 stitches (14 on each needle).

ROUNDS 15–17 Repeat Round 1 every round. *You now have* 32 stitches (8 on each needle).

ROUND 18 *Ssk twice, K2tog twice; repeat from * to end of round. *You now have* 16 stitches (4 on each needle).

ROUND 19 *Ssk, K2tog; repeat from * to end of round. *You now have* 8 stitches (2 on each needle).

Finishing

Cut working yarn, leaving a 10" (25 cm) tail. Thread tail into tapestry needle. Pull needle through all remaining stitches, drawstring-fashion, then pass through these stitches once again, draw up tight, and fasten off to close top of cap. Weave in ends.

Joining into a Round

If you have trouble making a firm join by simply beginning to knit, try joining your stitches into a round by trading places with the first and last cast-on stitches. Take the last cast-on stitch from Needle 4 and slide it onto Needle 1. Then take the first cast-on stitch from Needle 1 and slide it over the last stitch and onto Needle 4.

[He's Really Cute]
Mod Beanie

BEANIES ARE ALL THE RAGE, and if your new boyfriend likes to make a fashion statement, this will do the trick. The beanie is knitted in the current no-cuff style in oh-so-mod colors, but the best thing about it is that it's oh-so-simple to make. In fact, it's safe to knit this cap early on in the relationship.

To work Garter Stitch in the round, knit one row and purl the next.

The beanie has a decorative eight-point swirling decrease at the top.

YARN
Classic Elite Wings, 55% alpaca, 23% silk, 22% wool, approximately 109 yd (100 m)/50 g
Yarn band gauge: 4.75 stitches = 1" (2.5 cm) in stockinette stitch on US 7 (4.5 mm) needles
Color A: 2397 Woodland Green, 1 skein
Color B: 2310 Dark Navy, 1 skein
Color C: 2395 Sunset Purple, 1 skein

FINISHED SIZE
Approximately 20" (51 cm) around, unstretched, and 8" (20.5 cm) deep; will stretch up to 25" (63.5 cm) around

GAUGE
10.5 stitches = 2" in Pattern Stitch (Garter Stitch)

NEEDLES
Set of five US 7 (4.5 mm) double-pointed needles *or size you need to obtain the correct gauge*
Note: You may also use a US 7 (4.5mm) 16" (40 cm) circular needle until you get to the decrease rounds.

NOTIONS
Tapestry needle

ABBREVIATIONS
CA = Color A
CB = Color B
CC = Color C

pattern stitch

Garter Stitch

ROUND 1 Knit to end of round.

ROUND 2 Purl to end of round.

Repeat Rounds 1 and 2 for pattern.

Knitting the Hat

SET UP With CA, cast on 104 stitches. Place 26 stitches on each of four needles. Join into a round (see Joining into a Round, page 37). *Note:* Always change color before working Round 1 of Garter Stitch (a knit round).

NEXT ROUNDS Work CA in Garter Stitch for 1.5" (3 cm).

NEXT ROUNDS Work CB in Garter Stitch for 1.5" (3 cm).

NEXT ROUNDS Work CC in Garter Stitch for 1.5" (3 cm).

NEXT ROUNDS Work CA in Garter Stitch for 1.5" (3 cm).

Decreasing for Crown

SET UP Change to CB. *Note:* Always decrease on knit rounds.

ROUND 1 (KNIT ROUND) *K2tog, K11; repeat from * to end of round. You have just decreased 8 stitches (2 decreased on each needle).

ROUND 2 AND ALL EVEN-NUMBERED ROUNDS Work in Garter Stitch (purl).

ROUND 3 *K2tog, K10; repeat from * to end of round.

ROUND 5 *K2tog, K9; repeat from * to end of round.

ROUNDS 7–24 Continue as established, knitting one fewer stitch between decreases and working one purl round between decrease rounds, changing to CC after CB stripe is 1.5" (3 cm) wide. *You now have 8 stitches (2 on each needle).*

Finishing

Cut working yarn, leaving a 10" (25 cm) tail. Thread tail onto tapestry needle. Pull needle through all remaining stitches, drawstring-fashion, then pass through these stitches once again, draw up tight, and fasten off to close top of beanie. Weave in ends.

[Two Ways]
DIAMOND Headband

YOU CAN WORK THIS quick and rewarding project in either of two gauges for completely different looks. Is your guy big and bold? Knit the band in Lite-Lopi dark gray and white. Is he more understated? Knit it in Jaeger black and gray wool. If you knit it in Lite-Lopi, line the headband with synthetic fleece or a similar fabric so it won't be too itchy.

YARN
VERSION 1: Reynolds Lite-Lopi, 100% virgin wool, approximately 109 yd (99.5 m)/50 g
Yarn band gauge: 17 stitches = 4" (10 cm) in stockinette stitch on US 8 (5 mm) needles
Color A: 005 Charcoal, 1 ball
Color B: 0051 White, 1 ball
VERSION 2: Jaeger Extra Fine Merino DK, 100% merino wool, 136 yd (124.5 m)/50 g
Yarn band gauge: 22 stitches = 4" (10 cm) in stockinette stitch on US 5 or 6 (3.75 or 4.25 mm) needles
Color A: 951 Jet, 1 ball
Color B: 942 Flannel, 1 ball

FINISHED SIZE
VERSION 1: Approximately 21" (53.5 cm) around, unstretched, and 3.25" (8.5 cm) wide; will stretch up to 23.5" (59.5 cm) around
VERSION 2: Approximately 18" (45.5 cm) around, unstretched, and 3" (7.5 cm) wide; will stretch up to 23" (58.5 cm) around

GAUGE
VERSION 1: 8.5 stitches = 2" (5 cm) in Color Pattern
VERSION 2: 14.5 stitches = 2" (5 cm) in Color Pattern

NEEDLES
VERSION 1: One each 16" (40 cm) circular needle, US 7 and 8 (4.5 mm and 5 mm), *or sizes you need to obtain the correct gauge*
VERSION 2: One each 16" (40 cm) circular needle, US 5 and 6 (3.75 mm and 4 mm), *or sizes you need to obtain the correct gauge*

NOTIONS
Tapestry needle; for **VERSION 1**, 22" x 2.5" (56 cm x 6.5 cm) piece of synthetic fleece or similar lining material, sewing needle and coordinating thread for attaching lining, straight pins

ABBREVIATIONS
CA = Color A
CB = Color B

Knitting the Headband

Note: **VERSION 1** = Column 1 on the right; **VERSION 2** = Column 2 on the right.

SET UP With CA and smaller needle, cast on	90 sts	130 sts

Join into a round (see Joining into a Round, page 37), being careful not to twist stitches.

ROUNDS 1–4 Knit to end of round.

VERSION 2 only **ROUNDS 5–6** Knit to end of round.

NEXT ROUND Purl to end of round (turning ridge).

NEXT ROUND Change to larger needle, then knit to end of round.

Rounds of Color

When knitting in the round with two colors (color stranding), it's important to be consistent about which yarn goes over or under the other. The general rule is that the background color (in this case CA, the Charcoal or Jet) should go *over* the other strand, and the pattern color (in this case White or Flannel) should go *under* the other strand. Worked this way, the pattern strand stands out from the background, producing a more distinct design. The swatch at the top shows what happens when the pattern strand goes over the other strand. Notice that the diamonds are not as distinct and do not stand away from the background as clearly as those in the swatch at the bottom (from the headband in the photograph on page 42).

Working the Color Pattern

ROUND 1 AND NEXT ROUNDS Join CB and begin working
Color Pattern Chart below, beginning with Round 1
at bottom right. Work in Color Pattern for

	3" (7.5 cm)	2.5" (6.5 cm)
ending with Color Pattern Round	6	1

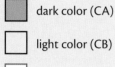

dark color (CA)

light color (CB)

Pattern repeat

Finishing

Change to smaller needle and CA.

ROUND 1 Knit to end of round.

ROUND 2 Purl to end of round (turning ridge).

ROUNDS 3–6 Knit to end of round.

VERSION 1 ONLY: Bind off all stitches loosely.

VERSION 2 ONLY **ROUNDS 7–8** Knit to end of round.

NEXT ROUND *K1, P1; repeat from * to end of round.

Repeat the last round until K1/P1 ribbing measures 2" (5 cm). Bind off all stitches loosely in ribbing. Using CA and tapestry needle, sew cast-on edge to bound-off edge.

BOTH VERSIONS Weave in ends with tapestry needle, wash, then block.

Lining (for Version 1)

Using a piece of fleece 22" (56 cm) long and 2.5" (6.5 cm) wide with right sides together, hand- or machine-sew together the two short ends, leaving 0.5" (1.25 cm) seam allowance.

With right sides of lining and headband touching, line up the cast-on edge of the knitted band with one long edge of the fleece. Pin in place, then hand-baste close to the edge. With a sewing machine or by hand, sew the pieces together with a scant ⅛" (3 mm) seam allowance. You should be sewing just inside the cast-on edge. Fold along this seam so that wrong sides are together.

Fold the other long edge of fleece ⅛" (3 mm) to wrong side and pin folded edge to knitted band just inside the bind-off edge. Whipstitch in place, being careful to sew only through fleece and one layer of knitting.

Alternative Start and Finish

The merino wool used for **VERSION 2** is soft enough to be worn without a fleece lining and has a ribbed inner face. For a seamless inside, begin with a Provisional Cast-On (see Techniques, page 176) and work as described above, but do not bind off. Continuing on the smaller needle, knit one round. Remove Provisional Cast-On and use Kitchener Stitch (see Techniques, page 179) to join the cast-on stitches to the live stitches on the needle.

[Let's Go Away for the Weekend]
Ski Hat

AN OVERNIGHTER? Ahem, things are getting serious. Here is a seriously great-looking hat that gives the appearance of being very complicated to knit but is actually quite simple. Knit at 10.5 stitches to the inch, however, it will be a bit time-consuming. Maybe you should wait until the weekend is over before casting on . . . or not casting on?

Using the Slip Stitch or Mosaic Colorwork Technique (see page 52), this hat is worked back and forth and is seamed up the back. The pattern is worked with an edge stitch at the beginning and end of each row, which will disappear into the seam. The hat features braided knitting and a contrasting pattern in the bottom band.

YARN
Dale of Norway Dalegarn Baby Ull, 100% machine-washable wool, 191 yd (175 m) per 50 g
Yarn band gauge: 32 stitches = 4" (10 cm) in stockinette stitch on US 1 (2.25 mm) needles
Color A = 5755 Navy, 2 skeins
Color B = 020 Off-White, 1 skein

FINISHED SIZE
21" (53.5 cm) around, unstretched, and 8" (20 cm) deep; will stretch up to 24" (61 cm) around

GAUGE
21 stitches = 2" (5 cm), unstretched, in Mosaic Pattern Stitch (Charts 1 and 2)

NEEDLES
US 1 (2.25 mm) *or size you need to obtain the correct gauge*

NOTIONS
Tapestry needle

ABBREVIATIONS
CA = Color A
CB = Color B

| pattern stitch |

Braid Stitch

(Even Number of Stitches)

ROW 1 (RIGHT SIDE) *K1 CA, K1 CB; repeat from *.

ROW 2 With both colors held in back for the entire row and bringing the new color over the old color for each stitch, *K1 CB, K1 CA; repeat from *.

ROW 3 With both colors held in front for the entire row and bringing the new color over the old color for each stitch, *P1 CA, P1 CB; repeat from *.

Note: The two yarns will twist around each other for each stitch as you work Row 2, but they will untwist when you work Row 3. If the twist becomes difficult to handle, cut a 5-yard (5 m) length of CB so that you can comb out the twist as you go along.

Knitting the Band

SET UP With CA, cast on 218 stitches.

ROWS 1 AND 2 Knit to end of row.

ROWS 3–5 Join CB and work Rows 1–3 of Braid Stitch.

ROW 6 With CA, purl to end of row.

ROWS 7–12 Knit to end of row.

ROWS 13–22 Referring to Slip Stitch or Mosaic Color Technique on page 52, work Rows 1–10 of Chart 1 (see page 51). *Note:* The first and last stitch of each row (edge stitches) is knit in the color that you are using in that row, not the color you are slipping. Each row of the chart represents two rows of knitting.

ROWS 23–28 With CA, knit to end of row.

ROWS 29–31 Join CB and work Rows 1–3 of Braid Stitch.

ROW 32 With CA, purl to end of row.

ROWS 33 AND 34 Knit to end of row. At this point, the piece should measure approximately 1.75" (4.5 cm) from the beginning.

Knitting the Mosaic Pattern

Referring to Slip Stitch or Mosaic Color Technique on page 52 and Chart 2 on page 53, work Rows 1–56 of Chart 2 two times, then work Rows 1–28 once more. ***Note:*** The first and last stitch of each row (edge stitches) is knit in the color that you are using in that row, not the color you are slipping. Each row of the chart represents two rows of knitting. At this point, piece should measure approximately 7.5" (19 cm) from the beginning.

Chart 1

Here's how you'll work the 8-stitch pattern repeat, including the edge stitches:

ROW 1 (CB) K1 CB (edge stitch), *K1 CB, slip 1 CA, K1 CB, slip 1 CA, K3 CB, slip 1 CA; repeat from * to last stitch, K1 CB (edge stitch).

ROW 2 (CB) K1 CB (edge stitch), *slip 1 CA, K3 CB, slip 1 CA, K1 CB, slip 1 CA, K1 CB; repeat from * to last stitch, K1 CB (edge stitch).

ROWS 3 AND 4 (CA) Knit all stitches with CA.

ROW 5 (CB) K1 CB (edge stitch), *K3 CB, slip 1 CA, K1 CB, slip 1 CA, K1 CB, slip 1 CA; repeat from * to last stitch, K1 CB (edge stitch).

ROW 6 (CB) K1 CB (edge stitch), *slip 1 CA, K1 CB, slip 1 CA, K1 CB, slip 1 CA, K3 CB; repeat from * to last stitch, end K1 CB (edge stitch).

ROWS 7 AND 8 (CA) Repeat Rows 3 and 4.

ROWS 9 AND 10 (CB) Repeat Rows 1 and 2.

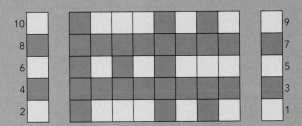

Finishing

ROWS 1–3 Work Rows 1–3 of Braid Stitch.

ROW 4 With CA, purl to end of row.

With CA, bind off all stitches.

Slip Stitch or Mosaic Color Technique

In this technique, all stitches are either knitted or slipped. Using two colors of yarn (dark — CA in this pattern — represented by a dark blue square on the chart, and light — CB in this pattern — represented by a light blue square), work all the way across one row and back again (two rows) in one color, then work the next two rows in the other color. When you are knitting with the dark yarn, you are slipping the light stitches, and vice versa. The second (even-numbered, wrong-side) row is a mirror image of the first — knit the stitches that you knitted and slip the stitches that you slipped in the row before. These second rows are not charted separately: Each line in the chart requires two rows of knitting with the same-color yarn.

The chart shows single edge stitches on both sides, separated a bit from the rest of the line. Whatever color you use for the edge stitches is the color you use to work that row and the next.

For each line of the chart, first work across a right-side row, knitting all the stitches in the color you are using and slipping all the stitches of the other color as if to purl. Following the same line of the chart, work a wrong-side row, knitting all the stitches shown in the color you are using and slipping the stitches in the other color as if to purl. *Note:* Bring the yarn to the front when slipping on wrong-side rows. For the next line of the chart, work two rows using the other color as indicated by the edge stitches, knitting the stitches shown in the new color and slipping stitches of the other color as described above.

Sew center-back seam using the invisible method (see Techniques, page 179). Mark center front, center back (seam line), and two midpoints between center front and center back. Now find the midpoints between these four points and bring together these midpoints at the center top of hat. Center front, center back, and the two midpoints between them now form the four points at the top of the hat. Invisibly sew the four short seams from the center out to each point (fig. 1).

Weave in ends with tapestry needle. Wash or steam, then block.

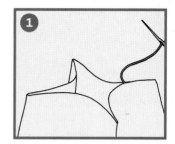

Chart 2

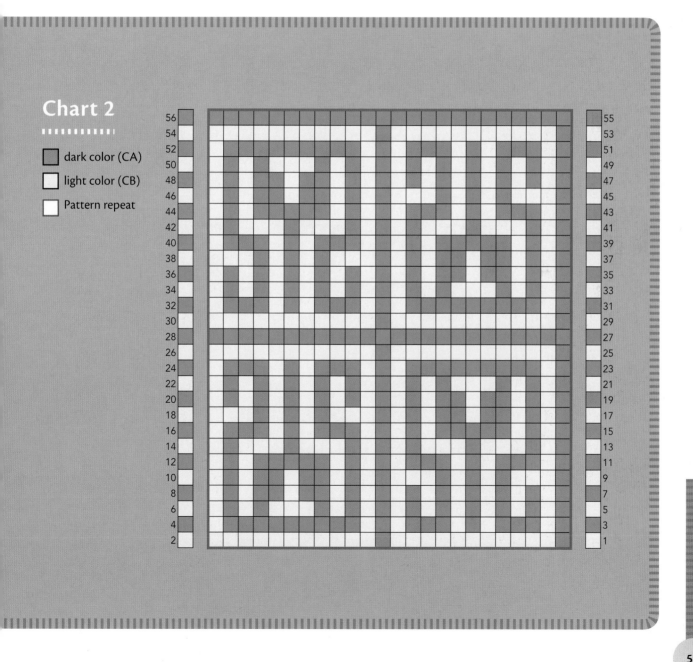

■ dark color (CA)

□ light color (CB)

□ Pattern repeat

[Let's Get Cozy]
PLAIN OLD Ragg Socks

IT'S FRIDAY NIGHT, the work week is behind you, and it's time for serious lounging. Put on your sweats, order your favorite take-out food, load a film in the DVD player, and get comfy together. These socks are great for padding around the house without shoes. (They're also perfect for wearing in work boots.)

This pattern is for a basic sock knitted in worsted-weight wool. A 1/1 rib (knit 1, purl 1) at the top keeps the sock up, and the Stockinette Stitch is easy to knit. Once you've mastered this sock, try substituting a 3/1 rib (knit 3, purl 1) for the top or another textured pattern for the Stockinette Stitch.

YARN
Patons Classic Merino Wool, 100% pure new wool, approximately 223 yd (204 m) per 100 g
Yarn band gauge: 20 stitches = 4" (10 cm) in Stockinette Stitch on US 7 (4.5 mm) needles
Color: 249 Stone Marl, 2 skeins

FINISHED SIZE
12" (30.5 cm) from cast-on edge to bottom of heel, 9.5" (24 cm) from back of heel to tip of toe

GAUGE
11 stitches = 2" in Pattern Stitch (Stockinette Stitch)

NEEDLES
Set of five US 7 (4.5 mm) double-pointed needles *or size you need to obtain the correct gauge*

NOTIONS
Tapestry needle, stitch holder (optional)

ABBREVIATIONS
ssk = slip one stitch, slip one stitch, knit the two stitches together through their back loops

pattern stitch

Stockinette Stitch

ROUND 1 Knit to end of round.

Repeat Round 1 for pattern.

Knitting the Cuff

SET UP Cast on 48 stitches. Place 12 stitches on each of four needles. Join into a round (see Joining into a Round, page 37), being careful not to twist stitches.

ROUND 1 *K1, P1; repeat from * to end of round.

NEXT ROUNDS Repeat Round 1 until piece measures 2" (5 cm).

Knitting the Leg

ROUND 1 Knit to end of round.

NEXT ROUNDS Work Stockinette Stitch until piece measures 8.5" (21.5 cm) or desired length from beginning to top of heel.

Knitting the Heel Flap

NOTE Slipping the first stitch of each row as if to purl in this section creates a neat edge that is easy to pick up: One stitch is formed at the edge for every two heel rows, making it easy to see which stitches to pick up later along the sides of the heel flap for the gussets.

SET UP K12, turn.

NEXT ROW (WRONG SIDE) Slip 1, P23. The 24 stitches just worked will form the heel flap. Leave remaining 24 stitches on the needles (or a stitch holder) to be used later for instep.

ROW 1 (RIGHT SIDE) *Slip 1 as if to purl with yarn held in back, K1; repeat from * to end of row.

ROW 2 Slip 1, P23.

ROWS 3–22 Repeat Rows 1 and 2 ten more times.

Turning the Heel

SET UP Slip 1, K14, ssk, turn. *You now have* 12 slipped stitches along each side of the heel flap.

ROW 1 (WRONG SIDE) Slip 1, P6, P2tog, turn.

ROW 2 Slip 1, K6, ssk, turn.

ROWS 3–15 Repeat Rows 1 and 2 six more times, then work Row 1 once more. All heel-flap stitches have been worked, and *you now have* 8 heel stitches.

NEXT ROW Knit across 8 heel stitches.

Knitting the Gussets

SET UP *Needle 1:* With the same needle that holds the 8 heel stitches (Needle 1), pick up and knit 12 stitches along the slipped-stitch edge of heel flap and 1 extra stitch in the corner between the heel flap and the instep stitches. (Picking up the extra stitch prevents a hole from forming at the join.)

Needles 2 and 3: Knit the stitches on Needles 2 and 3 that have been on hold (instep).

Needle 4: Pick up 1 extra stitch in the corner between the instep stitches and the heel flap, then pick up and knit 12 stitches along the other slipped-stitch edge of heel flap. With the same needle, knit the first 4 of the 8 heel stitches from Needle 1.

You now have 17 stitches each on Needles 1 and 4 and 12 stitches each on Needles 2 and 3, 58 stitches in total.

ROUND 1 *Needle 1:* Knit to last 2 stitches, K2tog.

Needles 2 and 3: Knit to end of needle.

Needle 4: Ssk, knit to end of needle.

ROUND 2 Knit to end of round.

NEXT ROUNDS Repeat Rounds 1 and 2 four more times. *You now have* 12 stitches on each needle, 48 stitches in total.

Knitting the Foot

Work even in Stockinette Stitch (knit to end of each round) until foot measures about 7.5" (19 cm), or approximately 2 inches (5 cm) less than desired finished foot length.

Shaping the Toe

ROUND 1 *Needle 1:* Knit to last 2 stitches, K2tog.

Needle 2: Ssk, knit to end of needle.

Needle 3: Knit to last 2 stitches, K2tog.

Needle 4: Ssk, knit to end of needle.

ROUND 2 Knit to end of round.

ROUNDS 3–10 Repeat Rounds 1 and 2 four more times. *You now have* 28 stitches.

ROUNDS 11–15 Repeat Round 1 only, without working a plain knit round in between the decrease rounds. *You now have* 8 stitches.

Finishing

Cut working yarn, leaving a 10" (25 cm) tail, and thread tail into a tapestry needle. Pull needle through all remaining stitches, drawstring-fashion, then pass through these stitches once again, draw up tight, and fasten off to close end of toe.

Weave in any loose ends with tapestry needle. Wash and block.

[Don't Put Them in the Dryer]
Socks

SOCKS ARE RELATIVELY EASY to make, and they're small enough that knitting a pair doesn't require a huge time investment. Remember, though, that once you've knit one, you have to knit the mate. And remember to tell him (repeatedly) not to put these socks in the washer or dryer!

Knit of Guernsey 5-ply, these socks should last a lifetime (as long as they never meet a dryer). The cable pattern is easy to remember, so you shouldn't have to refer to the instructions once you've turned a cable or two.

YARN
Wooly West Wendy Guernsey 5-ply, 100% wool, approximately 245 yd (224 m) per 100 g
Yarn band gauge: 28 stitches and 36 rows = 4" (10 cm) in stockinette stitch on US 1 to 3 (2.25 to 3 mm) needles
Color: Navy, 2 skeins

FINISHED SIZE
10.5" (26.5 cm) from cast-on edge to bottom of heel, 9.5" (24 cm) from back of heel to tip of toe

GAUGE
16 stitches = 2" (5 cm) in Pattern Stitch (Cable Pattern Stitch)

NEEDLES
Set of five US 3 (3 mm) double-pointed needles *or size you need to obtain the correct gauge*

NOTIONS
Cable needle, tapestry needle, stitch holder (optional)

ABBREVIATIONS
ssk = slip one stitch, slip one stitch, knit the two stitches together through their back loops

pattern stitch

Cable Pattern Stitch

▪▪▪▪▪▪▪▪▪▪

(Multiple of 16 Stitches. Work Once on Each of 4 Needles.)

ROUND 1 *K4, P1, slip next 3 stitches onto cable needle and hold in front, K3, K3 from cable needle, P1, K4; repeat from * to end of round.

ROUNDS 2–6 *K4, P1, K6, P1, K4; repeat from * to end of round.

Repeat Rounds 1–6 for pattern.

Knitting the Cuff

SET UP Cast on 64 stitches. Place 16 stitches on each of four needles. Join into a round (see Joining into a Round, page 37), being careful not to twist stitches.

ROUND 1 *K1, P1 to end of round.

NEXT ROUNDS Repeat Round 1 (1/1 ribbing) until piece measures 1.5" (4 cm).

Knitting the Leg

ROUNDS 1–6 Work Cable Pattern Stitch.

NEXT ROUNDS Repeat Rounds 1–6 of Cable Pattern Stitch until leg measures 7.5" (19 cm) or desired length to top of heel, ending with Round 1 of Cable Pattern Stitch.

Knitting the Heel Flap

NOTE Slipping the first stitch of each row as if to purl in this section creates a neat edge that is easy to pick up: One stitch is formed at the edge for every two heel rows, making it easy to see which stitches to pick up later along the sides of the heel flap for the gussets.

SET UP K16, turn.

NEXT ROW (WRONG SIDE) Slip 1, P31. The 32 heel stitches you have just worked will form the heel flap. Leave remaining 32 stitches on the needles (or a stitch holder) to be used later for instep.

ROW 1 (RIGHT SIDE) *Slip 1 as if to purl with yarn held in back, K1; repeat from * to end of row.

ROW 2 Slip 1, P31.

ROWS 3–30 Repeat Rows 1 and 2 fourteen more times.

Turning the Heel

SET UP *Slip 1, K1; repeat from * nine more times, slip 1, ssk, turn. *You now have* 16 slipped stitches along each side of the heel flap.

ROW 1 (WRONG SIDE) Slip 1, P11, P2tog, turn.

ROW 2 *Slip 1, K1; repeat from * four more times, slip 1, ssk, turn.

ROWS 3–19 Repeat Rows 1 and 2 eight more times, then work Row 1 once more. All heel-flap stitches have been worked, and *you now have* 12 heel stitches.

NEXT ROW Knit 12 heel stitches.

Knitting the Gussets

SET UP *Needle 1:* With the same needle that holds the 12 heel stitches (Needle 1), pick up and knit 16 stitches along the slipped-stitch edge of heel flap and 1 extra stitch in the corner between the heel-flap and the instep stitches. (Picking up the extra stitch prevents a hole from forming at the join.)

Needles 2 and 3: Work the stitches on hold on Needles 2 and 3 (instep) in established Cable Pattern Stitch; if you ended the leg with Round 1 of the pattern, you should resume by working Round 2 of the pattern.

Needle 4: Pick up 1 extra stitch in the corner between the instep stitches and the heel flap, then pick up and knit 16 edge stitches along the other slipped-stitch edge of heel flap. With the same needle, knit the first 6 of the 12 heel stitches from Needle 1. *You now have* 23 stitches each on Needles 1 and 4 and 16 stitches each on Needles 2 and 3, for 78 stitches in total.

ROUND 1 *Needle 1:* Knit to last 2 stitches, K2tog.

Needles 2 and 3: Work instep stitches in established Cable Pattern Stitch.

Needle 4: Ssk, knit to end of round.

ROUND 2 Knit all stitches on Needle 1, work in established pattern on 32 instep stitches on Needles 2 and 3, knit all stitches on Needle 4.

ROUNDS 3–14 Repeat Rounds 1 and 2 six more times. *You now have* 16 stitches on each needle, for 64 stitches in total.

Knitting the Foot

Work even as established (no further decreases on Needles 1 and 4), keeping the 32 instep stitches in Cable Pattern and working the remaining stitches in Stockinette Stitch, until foot measures 7.25" (18.5 cm), or approximately 2.25 inches (5.5 cm) less than desired finished foot length, ending with Round 1 of the Cable Pattern Stitch.

Shaping the Toe

ROUND 1 *Needle 1:* Knit to last 3 stitches, K2tog, K1.

Needle 2: K1, ssk, knit to end of needle.

Needle 3: Knit to last 3 stitches, K2tog, K1.

Needle 4: K1, ssk, knit to end of needle.

ROUND 2 Knit to end of round.

ROUNDS 3–16 Repeat Rounds 1 and 2 seven more times. *You now have* 32 stitches.

ROUNDS 17–19 Repeat decrease Round 1 three times without working the plain Round 2 in between the decrease rounds. *You now have* 20 stitches.

ROUND 20 Repeat Round 1. At the same time, knit the stitches from Needle 3 onto Needle 2 and knit the first 4 stitches from Needle 1 onto Needle 4. *You now have* 16 stitches, 8 stitches each on two needles.

Finishing

Holding the two needles parallel with the wrong sides of the work touching, use Kitchener Stitch (see Techniques, page 179) to graft together the toe stitches.

Weave in any loose ends with tapestry needle. Wash and block.

[Okay, I'll Wash Them]
DIAMOND Socks

ARGYLE IS CLASSIC. Around since the 1920s, it has been in and out of fashion, but now it's most definitely in, so it's a great idea to incorporate the pattern into socks. That said, this pair takes both brain power and time, so under no circumstances should your boyfriend have the opportunity to throw these socks into the washer and dryer with the rest of his laundry. If you want to knit these socks, consider protecting your investment by committing to care for them.

This pattern is based on one that was originally published by Bucilla Yarn in 1950 and is used by permission of Plaid Enterprises. The patterned leg is knit back and forth and is seamed up the back. The stitches are then joined and the foot and toe are worked in the round.

YARN
Rowan 4-Ply Soft, 100% merino wool, approximately 191 yd (175 m) per 50 g
Yarn band gauge: 31 stitches = 4" (10 cm) in stockinette stitch on US 1 or 2 (2.25 or 2.5 mm) needles
Color A = 367 Leafy (green), 2 skeins; alternative color: 372 Sooty (dark gray)
Color B = 392 Sandalwood (salmon), 1 skein; alternative color: 380 Marine (navy)
Color C = 393 Linseed (beige), 1 skein; alternative color: 387 Rain Cloud (light gray)
Color D = 379 Goblin (light green), 20 yards; alternative color: 385 Puff (beige)

FINISHED SIZE
11.5" (29 cm) from cast-on edge of top to bottom of heel, 9.5" (24 cm) from back of heel to tip of toe

GAUGE
18 stitches = 2" (5 cm) in Argyle Color Chart Pattern (page 69)

NEEDLES
Set of four or five US 2 (2.75 mm) double-pointed needles *or size you need to obtain the correct gauge*

NOTIONS
Tapestry needle, stitch holders, yarn bobbins (optional). *Note:* You may choose between these two methods of working with two colors: (1) Wind each color onto separate bobbins that hang off the back of your work when not in use (you will need a separate bobbin for each block of color in the row) or (2) cut long lengths of each color, then, from the rat's nest that develops as you work, pull what you need for each row. It takes approximately 15 yds (14 m) to knit one diamond.

ABBREVIATIONS
CA = Color A
CB = Color B
CC = Color C
CD = Color D

ssk = slip one stitch, slip one stitch, knit the two stitches together through their back loops

Knitting the Cuff

SET UP Using CA, loosely cast on 68 stitches. Place 34 stitches on each of two needles and work all stitches back and forth in rows; do not join for working in the round.

ROW 1 (RIGHT SIDE) *K2, P2; repeat from * to end of row (2/2 rib).

NEXT ROWS Repeat Row 1 until piece measures 3" (7.5 cm), increasing 7 stitches evenly spaced in the last row of rib. *You now have* 75 stitches.

Knitting the Leg

ROW 1 (SETUP; ALSO ROW 1 OF ARGYLE COLOR CHART, PAGE 69) Join CC, K1.

With CA, K17.

Join CD, K1.

Join another strand of CD, K1.

With CA, K17.

Join CB, K1.

Join another strand of CA, K17.

Join another strand of CD, K1.

Join another strand of CD, K1.

With CA, K17.

Join another strand of CC, K1.

ROWS 2–74 Continue working Argyle Color Chart Pattern in Stockinette Stitch (knit the right-side rows, purl the wrong-side rows).

ROW 75 With CA, K19, then place the stitches just worked on holder for heel. Work next 37 stitches in pattern. Place remaining 19 stitches on holder for heel.

ROWS 76–101 Continue in Argyle Color Chart pattern on 37 stitches to end of chart.

Place stitches on holder for top of foot.

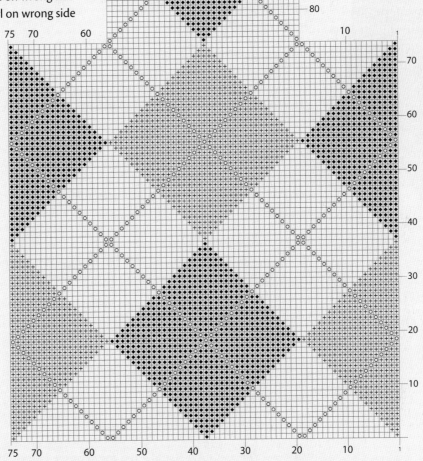

Knitting the Heel Flap

SET UP Place 38 held heel stitches on a single needle with side edges of the leg at center of needle. With wrong side facing you, join CA.

ROW 1 (WRONG SIDE) Slip 1 purlwise, purl to end of row.

ROW 2 *Slip 1 purlwise, K1; repeat from * to end of row.

ROWS 3–36 Repeat Rows 1 and 2 seventeen more times.

Color A: knit on right side; purl on wrong side
Color B: knit on right side; purl on wrong side
Color C: knit on right side; purl on wrong side
Color D: knit on right side; purl on wrong side

Turning the Heel

ROW 1 (WRONG SIDE) Slip 1, P20, P2tog, P1, turn.

ROW 2 Slip 1, K5, ssk, K1, turn.

ROW 3 Slip 1, P6, P2tog, P1, turn.

ROW 4 Slip 1, K7, ssk, K1, turn.

ROWS 5–16 Continue in this manner, working one more stitch before decrease on each row, until you have worked all stitches. *You now have* 22 stitches. Break CA.

Knitting the Gussets

NOTE The gussets are worked flat, back and forth in rows, on two needles; you do not begin working the sock in the round until the next section, Knitting the Foot.

SET UP *Needle 1:* Rejoin CA to the base of the heel flap with right side facing you. With new needle, pick up and knit 18 stitches along slipped-stitch edge of heel flap, then knit the first 11 heel stitches onto the same needle.

Needle 2: With new needle, knit the remaining 11 heel stitches, then pick up and knit 18 stitches along the other slipped-stitch edge of heel flap. *You now have* 58 stitches, 29 stitches on each of two needles.

ROW 1 (WRONG SIDE) Purl to end of each needle.

ROW 2 *Needle 1:* K1, ssk, knit to end of needle.

Needle 2: Knit to last 3 stitches, K2tog, K1.

ROWS 3–22 Repeat Rows 1 and 2 ten more times. *You now have* 36 stitches, 18 stitches each on two needles. Place all stitches on one needle for sole of foot.

ROWS 23–37 Work even in Stockinette Stitch across all stitches, ending with a wrong-side purl row.

Knitting the Foot

SET UP Divide the 36 sole stitches onto two needles, placing 18 stitches each on Needles 1 and 3, and place 37 held instep stitches on Needle 2. *You now have* 73 stitches. Join for working in the round.

ROUND 1 Knit to end of round, decreasing one stitch at center of Needle 2 (instep). *You now have* 72 stitches.

NEXT ROUNDS Knit to the end of each round until foot measures 7.5" (19 cm), or 2 inches (5 cm) less than desired finished length. End at the center of the sole at the beginning of Needle 1.

Shaping the Toe

ROUND 1 *Needle 1:* Knit to last 3 stitches, K2tog, K1.

Needle 2: K1, ssk, knit to last 3 stitches, K2tog, K1.

Needle 3: K1, ssk, knit to end of needle.

ROUND 2 Knit to end of each needle.

ROUNDS 3–26 Repeat Rounds 1 and 2 twelve more times. *You now have* 20 stitches.

ROUND 27 K5 on Needle 1, then slip these to Needle 3; there will be 10 stitches each on two needles. Use Kitchener Stitch (see Techniques, page 179) to join together remaining stitches.

Finishing

Sew back seam, matching pattern (Seaming without Edge Stitches, below). Sew gusset seams at each side of foot.

Weave in tails, using them to tighten up any loose areas at the color changes as necessary. Wash and block.

Seaming without Edge Stitches

The technique for seaming when you don't have edge stitches to "lose" in the seam is the same as when you do (see Techniques, page 179), except that you pick up only half a stitch, instead of a full stitch, on each side of the seam.

[Protect His Hands] Mittens

THERE IS NOTHING WORSE THAN DRY CHAPPED HANDS in winter, especially if those hands are holding yours! Here's a very basic mitten pattern that can be knit up in his favorite color using any number of different yarns. You may also add a cable or other textured pattern to the backs or knit the mittens in stripes.

They are knit with thumbs slightly offset from the side "seam." You could also put the thumbs directly at the side and make them ambidextrous, but where's the challenge in that? They also fit better this way.

YARN
Classic Elite Wings, 55% alpaca, 23% silk, 22% wool, approximately 109 yd (99.5 m) per 50 g
Yarn band gauge: 4.75 stitches = 1" (2.5 cm) in stockinette stitch on US 7 (4.5 mm) needles
Color: 2313 Black, 2 skeins

FINISHED SIZE
Approximately 10.5" (26.5 cm) from cast-on edge of cuff to top of hand and 8.5" (21.5 cm) hand circumference

GAUGE
11 stitches = 2" (5 cm) in Pattern Stitch (Stockinette Stitch)

NEEDLES
Set of five US 6 (4 mm) double-pointed needles *or size you need to obtain the correct gauge*

NOTIONS
Stitch holder, tapestry needle, stitch markers

ABBREVIATIONS
M1 = make 1 increase (see Techniques, page 181)

pattern
stitch

**Stockinette
Stitch**

ıııııııı

ROUND 1 Knit to end
of round.

Repeat Round 1 for
pattern.

Right Mitten

Knitting the Cuff

SET UP Cast on 48 stitches. Place 12 stitches on each of four needles. Join into a round (see Joining into a Round, page 37), being careful not to twist stitches.

ROUND 1 *K1, P1; repeat from * to end of round.

NEXT ROUNDS Repeat Round 1 (1/1 rib) until piece measures 3" (7.5 cm) or desired length of cuff.

Knitting the Hand

SET UP FOR THUMB GORE On Needle 1, place markers after the third and fourth stitches; the fourth stitch from the beginning of Needle 1 should have a marker on each side of the stitch.

ROUNDS 1 AND 2 Knit to end of round in Stockinette Stitch.

ROUND 3 Knit to first marker, slip marker, M1, K1, M1, slip second marker, knit to end of round. *You now have* 3 thumb-gore stitches between markers.

ROUNDS 4 AND 5 Knit to end of round.

ROUND 6 Knit to first marker, slip marker, M1, knit to second marker, M1, slip second marker, knit to end of round. *You now have* 5 thumb-gore stitches between markers.

ROUNDS 7–23 Repeat Rounds 4–6 five more times, then work Rounds 4 and 5 again. *You now have* 15 thumb stitches between markers.

ROUNDS 24 AND 25 Knit to end of round.

ROUND 26 Knit to first marker, place 15 thumb stitches on a holder, remove marker, cast on 1 stitch, knit to end of round. *You now have* 48 stitches.

NEXT ROUNDS Work even until piece measures 6" (15 cm) from end of ribbing, or 1.5 inches (4 cm) less than desired length to tip of longest finger.

Decreasing for the Top

ROUND 1 *K4, K2tog; repeat from * to end of round. *You now have* 40 stitches.

ROUND 2 Knit to end of round.

ROUND 3 *K3, K2tog; repeat from * to end of round. *You now have* 32 stitches.

ROUND 4 Knit to end of round.

ROUND 5 *K2, K2tog; repeat from * to end of round. *You now have* 24 stitches.

ROUND 6 Knit to end of round.

ROUND 7 *K1, K2tog; repeat from * to end of round. *You now have* 16 stitches.

ROUND 8 Knit to end of round.

ROUND 9 *K2tog; repeat from * to end of round. *You now have* 8 stitches.

Cut working yarn, leaving a 10" (25.5 cm) tail, and thread tail into a tapestry needle. Pull needle through all remaining stitches, drawstring-fashion, then pass through these stitches once again, draw up tight, and fasten off to close top of mitten.

Weave in the end.

Knitting the Thumb

SET UP Divide the 15 thumb-gore stitches among three needles as follows.

Needle 1: 6 stitches

Needle 2: 6 stitches

Needle 3: 3 stitches, then with this needle pick up and knit 5 stitches for thumb gore along the top edge of the thumb hole. Decrease the first and last of these 5 stitches on the next round (see No Holes, below). *You now have* 18 stitches.

ROUND 1 Knit to end of round.

NEXT ROUNDS Continue in Stockinette Stitch until thumb measures 2" (5 cm) or 0.5 inches (1.3 cm) less than desired length.

No Holes

In making the thumbs of mittens, you need to knit with two more stitches than the number you cast on after placing the thumb-gusset stitches on hold. These two stitches are picked up on either side of the cast-on stitch. But to prevent holes from forming at the base of thumbs and fingers in mittens and gloves, pick up an extra stitch on each side of the stitch or stitches you'll be working for the thumb or a finger. When you work the next round, knit the first extra stitch together with the stitch before it, and the second extra stitch together with the stitch after it.

Decreasing for Top of Thumb

ROUND 1 *K1, K2tog; repeat from * to end of round. *You now have* 12 stitches.

ROUND 2 K2tog to end of round. *You now have* 6 stitches.

ROUND 3 Repeat Round 2. *You now have* 3 stitches.

Finishing

Cut working yarn, leaving a 10" (25.5 cm) tail, and thread tail into a tapestry needle. Close top of thumb as you did top of mitten.

Weave in any loose ends, using the tail at the base of the thumb to close up any holes that have appeared despite your best efforts.

Left Mitten

Work as for Right Mitten, *except* when you set up for the thumb gore (the first step in the instruction for Knitting the Hand, page 74), place the markers after the eighth and ninth stitches on Needle 2; the fourth stitch from the end of Needle 2 should have a marker on each side of the stitch.

[He's Driving Me Wild] Gloves

UNLIKE MITTENS, gloves require that you isolate stitches and knit ten fingers (actually, two thumbs and eight fingers). If you're going to take the time to do this, use the best yarn you can afford, like this delicious cashmere and merino blend.

Knit with a handsome cable and an extra-long cuff that your boyfriend can fold down or wear up for added protection, these gloves feature Seed Stitch on the palms and palm side of the fingers for added traction on a steering wheel.

YARN

Lana Grossa Pashmina, 22% cashmere, 78% merino extrafine, 136 yd (125 m) per 50 g

Yarn band gauge: 20 stitches and 26 rows = 4" (10 cm) in stockinette stitch on US 7 (4.5 mm) or US 8 (5 mm) needles

Color: 10 Maroon, 2 skeins

FINISHED SIZE

12" (30.5 cm) from cast-on edge of cuff to tip of middle finger, 8" (20.5 cm) hand circumference

GAUGE

12 stitches = 2" (5 cm) in Stockinette Stitch

NEEDLES

Set of four US 4 (3.5 mm) double-pointed needles *or size you need to obtain the correct gauge*

NOTIONS

Cable needle, 3 stitch markers, tapestry needle

ABBREVIATIONS

M1 = make 1 increase (see Techniques, page 181)

Left Glove

SET UP Cast on 50 stitches and distribute them among three needles as follows.

Needles 1 and 2: 16 stitches each.

Needle 3: 18 stitches.

ROUND 1 *K1, P1; repeat from * to end of round.

NEXT ROUNDS Repeat Round 1 (1/1 rib) until piece measures 5" (12.5 cm).

NEXT ROUND *Needle 1:* Knit to end of needle, then knit the first stitch from Needle 2 onto Needle 1. On Needle 1, *you now have* 17 stitches.

Needle 2: K8, place marker, knit to end of needle. On Needle 2, *you now have* 15 stitches.

Needle 3: Knit to end of needle.

NOTE The back of the glove begins at stitch 1 on Needle 1; the palm begins after the marker on Needle 2.

---

pattern stitch

Cable Pattern Stitch

(Worked over 25 Stitches)

ROUND 1 K6, P2, K9, P2, K6.

ROUND 2 Repeat Round 1.

ROUND 3 K6, P2, slip 3 stitches to cable needle and hold in front, K3, K3 from cable needle, K3, P2, K6.

ROUNDS 4, 5, AND 6 Repeat Round 1.

ROUND 7 K6, P2, K3, slip 3 stitches to cable needle and hold in back, K3, K3 from cable needle, P2, K6.

ROUND 8 Repeat Round 1.

Repeat Rounds 1–8 for pattern.

pattern stitch

Seed Stitch

▪▪▪▪▪▪▪▪▪▪▪▪

(Odd Number of Stitches)

ROUND 1 *K1, P1; repeat from * to last stitch, end K1.

ROUND 2 *P1, K1; repeat from * to last stitch, end P1.

Repeat Rounds 1 and 2 for pattern.

pattern stitch

Seed Stitch

▪▪▪▪▪▪▪▪▪▪▪▪

(Even Number of Stitches)

ROUND 1 *K1, P1; repeat from * to end of round.

ROUND 2 *P1, K1; repeat from * to end of round.

Repeat Rounds 1 and 2 for pattern.

Knitting the Back, Palm, and Thumb Gore

ROUND 1 Work Cable Pattern Stitch Round 1 over the first 25 stitches (Back); slip marker. Work Seed Stitch over an odd number of stitches to 4 stitches from end of Needle 3, place first marker for thumb gore, K1, place second marker for thumb gore, K3.

ROUND 2 Work Cable Pattern Stitch Round 2 over 25 Back stitches; slip marker. Work Seed Stitch to first thumb-gore marker, slip marker, M1, K1, M1, slip second thumb-gore marker, K3. *You now have* 3 thumb-gore stitches between markers.

ROUND 3 Work Cable Pattern Stitch Round 3 over 25 Back stitches; slip marker. Work Seed Stitch to marker, slip marker, knit across thumb-gore stitches, slip marker, K3.

ROUND 4 Repeat Round 3, working Cable Pattern Stitch Round 4.

ROUND 5 Work Cable Pattern Stitch Round 5 over 25 Back stitches; slip marker. Work Seed Stitch to marker, slip marker, M1, knit to second thumb-gore marker, M1, slip marker, K3. *You now have* 5 stitches between thumb-gore markers.

ROUNDS 6–20 Repeat Rounds 3–5 five more times, continuing and repeating eight-row Cable Pattern Stitch as established. *You now have* 15 thumb stitches between markers.

ROUND 21 Work Cable Pattern Stitch over 25 Back stitches, slip marker. Work Seed Stitch to marker, slip marker, work first thumb-gore stitch in Seed Stitch, knit the next 14 thumb-gore stitches, slip marker, K3.

ROUND 22 Repeat Round 21.

ROUND 23 Work Cable Pattern Stitch over 25 Back stitches, slip marker. Work Seed Stitch to marker, slip marker, M1, work 1 stitch Seed Stitch, K14, M1, slip marker, K3. *You now have* 17 thumb-gore stitches.

ROUND 24 (ROUND 8 OF CABLE PATTERN STITCH) Work Cable Pattern Stitch over 25 Back stitches, slip marker. Work Seed Stitch to marker, slip marker, work 3 stitches of thumb gore in Seed Stitch, K14, slip marker, K3.

ROUND 25 Work Cable Pattern Stitch over 25 Back stitches, slip marker. Work Seed Stitch to next marker. Place 17 thumb stitches on holder. Cast on 1 stitch, K3. *You now have* 50 stitches.

ROUNDS 26–40 Continue even in patterns as established, working Cable Pattern Stitch for the first 25 stitches, Seed Stitch for the next 22 stitches, and Stockinette Stitch for the last 3 stitches. You have completed two more eight-round repeats of the Cable Pattern Stitch, for a total of five repeats.

Shaping Fingers

NOTE From here on, discontinue Cable Pattern Stitch over Back and work all Back stitches in Stockinette Stitch. Continue Seed Stitch on Palm, ending each round with 3 stockinette stitches as established.

You may find it easier to use short lengths of yarn as string holders when placing stitches on hold for the fingers.

ROUND 1 K19 Back stitches. Place next 6 Back stitches on a string holder for the little finger. Remove marker and place the first 5 Palm stitches on a string holder for the little finger. Cast on 3 stitches over the gap where the little-finger stitches were removed, rejoin into a round, and work Palm stitches to end in Seed Stitch and Stockinette Stitch as established. *You now have* 42 stitches.

ROUNDS 2–5 Work even, keeping new cast-on stitches in Stockinette Stitch.

Knitting the Ring Finger

SET UP Knit 13 Back stitches and place on string holder. K9 to end of new cast-on stitches, work next 6 Seed Stitches, place remaining 14 Palm stitches on string holder, cast on 3 stitches, join into round. *You now have* 18 Ring Finger stitches.

NEXT ROUNDS Work in the round, keeping 6 stitches on Palm side of finger in Seed Stitch as established and working remaining stitches in Stockinette Stitch, until Ring Finger measures 2.5" (6.5 cm) or 0.25 inch (0.5 cm) less than desired length.

NEXT ROUND *K2tog, K1; repeat from * to end of round. *You now have* 12 stitches.

NEXT ROUND *K2tog; repeat from * to end of round. *You now have* 6 stitches.

Cut working yarn, leaving a 4" (10 cm) tail, and thread tail into a tapestry needle. Pull needle through remaining stitches, drawstring-fashion, then pass through these stitches once again, draw up tight, and fasten off to close top of finger.

Knitting the Middle Finger

SET UP Place on needle 6 of the Back stitches that are closest to the ring finger. With new yarn at end of needle, pick up and knit 3 stitches from base of Ring Finger (see No Holes, page 76), place next 6 Palm stitches on needle, work across them in established Seed Stitch, cast on 3 stitches, join into round, K6 Back stitches. *You now have* 18 Middle Finger stitches.

NEXT ROUNDS Work in the round, keeping 6 stitches on Palm side of finger in Seed Stitch as established and working remaining stitches in Stockinette Stitch, until Middle Finger measures 2.75" (7 cm) or 0.25 inch (0.5 cm) less than desired length. Finish as for Ring Finger.

Knitting the Index Finger

SET UP Place 8 Palm and 7 Back stitches on needle. With new yarn at end of Back stitches, pick up and knit 3 stitches from base of Middle Finger (see No Holes, page 76). Join into round. *You now have* 18 Index Finger stitches.

NEXT ROUNDS Work in the round, keeping 5 stitches on Palm side of finger in Seed Stitch as established and working remaining stitches in Stockinette Stitch until Index Finger measures 2.5" (6.5 cm) or 0.25 inch (0.5 cm) less than desired length. Finish as for Ring Finger.

Knitting the Little Finger

SET UP Place 5 Palm and 6 Back stitches on needle. With new yarn at end of Palm stitches, pick up and knit 3 stitches from base of Ring Finger (see No Holes, page 76). Join into round. *You now have* 14 Little Finger stitches.

NEXT ROUNDS Work in the round, keeping 5 stitches on Palm side of finger in Seed Stitch as established and working remaining stitches in Stockinette Stitch until Little Finger measures 2" (5 cm) or 0.25 inch (0.5 cm) less than desired length.

NEXT ROUND *K2tog, K1; repeat from * three more times, K2tog. *You now have* 9 stitches.

NEXT ROUND K2tog four times, K1. *You now have* 5 stitches.

Close top of Little Finger as for other fingers.

Knitting the Thumb

SET UP Place 17 Thumb stitches on two needles with the 3 Seed Stitches at the beginning of the first needle. With new yarn at end of Thumb stitches, pick up and knit 3 stitches from the stitches cast on over thumb hole (see No Holes, page 76). Join into round. *You now have* 20 Thumb stitches.

NEXT ROUNDS Work in the round, keeping 3 picked-up stitches and 3 stitches on inner edge of thumb in Seed Stitch as established, until thumb measures 1.75" (4.5 cm) or 0.25 inch (0.5 cm) less than desired length.

NEXT ROUND *K2tog, K1; repeat from * five more times, K2tog. *You now have* 13 stitches.

NEXT ROUND K2tog six times, K1. *You now have* 7 stitches.

Close top of Thumb as for other fingers.

Right Glove

Work as for Left Glove until 5" (12.5 cm) of rib and the first round after the rib have been completed. *You now have* 17 stitches on Needle 1, 15 stitches on Needle 2, and 18 stitches on Needle 3.

NOTE The Palm of the glove begins at stitch 1 on Needle 1; the Back begins after the marker on Needle 2.

Knitting the Back, Palm, and Thumb Gore

ROUND 1 K3, place first marker for thumb gore, K1, place second marker for thumb gore, work Seed Stitch to next marker, slip marker. Work Cable Pattern Stitch over the last 25 stitches (Back).

ROUND 2 K3, slip marker, M1, K1, M1, slip second thumb-gore marker, work Seed Stitch to next marker, slip marker. Work Cable Pattern Stitch over 25 Back stitches. *You now have* 3 thumb-gore stitches between markers.

ROUND 3 K3, slip marker, knit across thumb-gore stitches, slip marker, work Seed Stitch to marker, slip marker. Work Cable Pattern Stitch over 25 Back stitches.

ROUND 4 Repeat Round 3.

ROUND 5 K3, slip marker, M1, knit to second thumb-gore marker, M1, slip marker, work Seed Stitch to next marker, slip marker. Work Cable Pattern Stitch over 25 Back stitches. *You now have* 5 stitches between thumb-gore markers.

ROUNDS 6–20 Repeat Rounds 3–5 five more times. *You now have* 15 thumb stitches between markers.

ROUND 21 K3, slip marker, K14, work 1 stitch in Seed Stitch, slip marker, work Seed Stitch to next marker, slip marker. Work Cable Pattern Stitch over 25 Back stitches.

ROUND 22 Repeat Round 21.

ROUND 23 K3, slip marker, M1, K14, work 1 stitch in Seed Stitch, M1, slip marker, work Seed Stitch to next marker, slip marker. Work Cable Pattern Stitch over 25 Back stitches. *You now have* 17 thumb-gore stitches.

ROUND 24 (ROUND 8 OF CABLE PATTERN STITCH) K3, slip marker, K14, work 3 stitches in Seed Stitch, slip marker, work Seed Stitch to next marker. Work Cable Pattern Stitch over 25 Back stitches.

ROUND 25 K3, place 17 thumb stitches on holder, removing markers. Cast on 1 stitch. Work Seed Stitch to next marker. Work Cable Pattern Stitch over 25 Back stitches. *You now have* 50 stitches.

ROUNDS 26–40 Continue even in patterns as established, Stockinette Stitch for the first 3 stitches, Seed Stitch for the next 22 stitches, and Cable Pattern Stitch for the last 25 stitches. You have completed two more eight-round repeats of the Cable Pattern Stitch for a total of five repeats.

Shaping Fingers

NOTE From here on, discontinue Cable Pattern Stitch over Back and work all Back stitches in Stockinette Stitch. Continue Seed Stitch on Palm, beginning each round with the 3 Stockinette Stitches as established.

You may find it easier to use short lengths of yarn as string holders when placing stitches on hold for the fingers.

ROUND 1 Work 20 Palm stitches in Seed Stitch. Place next 5 Palm stitches on a string holder for the little finger. Remove marker and place the first 6 Back stitches on a string holder for the little finger. Cast on 3 stitches over the gap where the Little Finger stitches were removed, rejoin into a round, and work Back stitches in Stockinette Stitch to end. *You now have* 42 stitches.

ROUNDS 2–5 Work even, keeping newly cast-on stitches in Stockinette Stitch.

Knitting the Ring Finger

SET UP Work 14 Palm stitches in Seed Stitch and place on a string holder. Work next 6 Seed Stitches, K9, place remaining 13 Back stitches on a string holder, cast on 3 stitches, join into round. *You now have* 18 Ring Finger stitches.

Complete as for Left Glove Ring Finger.

Knitting the Middle Finger

SET UP Place on needle 6 Palm stitches closest to the ring finger. With new yarn at end of needle, pick up and knit 3 stitches from base of Ring Finger (see No Holes, page 76), place next 6 Back stitches on needle and knit them, cast on 3 stitches, join into round, work 6 Palm stitches in Seed Stitch. *You now have* 18 Middle Finger stitches.

Complete as for Left Glove Middle Finger.

Knitting the Index Finger

SET UP Place 8 Palm and 7 Back stitches on needle. With new yarn at end of Palm stitches, pick up and knit 3 stitches from base of Middle Finger (see NoHoles, page 76). Join into round. *You now have* 18 Index Finger stitches.

Complete as for Left Glove Index Finger.

Knitting the Little Finger

SET UP Place 5 Palm and 6 Back stitches on needle. With new yarn at end of Back stitches, pick up and knit 3 stitches from base of Ring Finger (see No Holes, page 76). Join into round. *You now have* 14 Little Finger stitches.

Complete as for Left Glove Ring Finger.

Knitting the Thumb

SET UP Place 17 Thumb stitches on two needles with the 3 Seed Stitches at the end of the second needle. With new yarn at end of Thumb stitches, pick up and knit 3 stitches from stitches cast on over thumb hole (see No Holes, page 76). Join into round. *You now have* 20 Thumb stitches.

Complete as for Left Glove Thumb.

Finishing

Weave in all loose ends, using tails to close up any holes that formed despite your best efforts. Wash or steam, then block.

[Flip Your Lid]
DIAMOND Mittens

HERE'S A VERSATILE ITEM that makes it easy for your boyfriend to free his fingers with a simple flip of the "lid" that serves as the top of these mittens. Whether he needs to fish around for some change, use his key to unlock the door, or simply touch you on the cheek, he can do so easily with these in the "mitten flipped" position.

The lid overlaps the under mitt by several stitches on each side for added protection, and the decreases for the top of the mitten follow the lines of the diamond pattern. The instructions are for knitted fingers that end just before the first knuckle, but you can knit them a little longer if you'd like.

YARN
Norwegian Spirit Lanett Super-
    wash, 100% merino wool,
    213 yd (195 m) per 50 g
Yarn band gauge: 31 stitches
    = 4" (10 cm) in Stockinette
    Stitch on US 1 or 2 (2.25
    or 2.5 mm) needles
Color: 1032 Gray, 2 skeins

FINISHED SIZE
9.5" (24 cm) from cast-on
    edge of cuff to top of hand;
    8.5" (21.5 cm) hand
    circumference

GAUGE
18 stitches = 2" (5 cm) in
    Stockinette Stitch

NEEDLES
Set of five US 1 (2.25 mm)
    double-pointed needles *or
    size you need to obtain the
    correct gauge*

NOTIONS
Stitch holder, tapestry needle,
    stitch markers

ABBREVIATIONS
M1 = make 1 increase
    (see Techniques, page 181)
ssk = slip one stitch, slip one
    stitch, knit the two stitches
    together through their back
    loops

Diamond Pattern Stitch

(Multiple of 8 Stitches Plus 1)

ROUND 1 *P1, K7; repeat from * to last stitch, P1.

ROUND 2 *K1, P1, K5, P1; repeat from * to last stitch, K1.

ROUND 3 *K2, P1, K3, P1, K1; repeat from * to last stitch, K1.

ROUND 4 *K3, P1, K1, P1, K2; repeat from * to last stitch, K1.

ROUND 5 *K4, P1, K3; repeat from * to last stitch, K1.

ROUND 6 Repeat Round 4.

ROUND 7 Repeat Round 3.

ROUND 8 Repeat Round 2.

Repeat Rounds 1–8 for pattern.

Left Mitten

Knitting the Cuff

SET UP Cast on 72 stitches. Place 18 stitches on each of four needles. Join into a round (see Joining into a Round, page 37), being careful not to twist stitches.

ROUND 1 *K2, P2; repeat from * to end of round.

NEXT ROUNDS Repeat Round 1 (2/2 rib) until piece measures 2.5" (6.5 cm).

NEXT ROUND Increase 1 stitch and knit to end of round. *You now have* 73 stitches.

Knitting the Hand

SET UP Redistribute stitches for Palm (Needles 1 and 2) and Back (Needles 3 and 4) as follows.

Needles 1 and 2: 16 stitches on each needle

Needle 3: 20 stitches

Needle 4: 21 stitches

NOTE Throughout this section, work Palm stitches on Needles 1 and 2 in Stockinette Stitch (knit all stitches every round) and work 41 Back stitches on Needles 3 and 4 in Diamond Pattern Stitch.

ROUND 1 (FIRST INCREASE ROUND FOR THUMB) K31 (Palm), M1, place marker, K1 (center thumb stitch), place marker, M1, work 41 stitches in Diamond Pattern Stitch.

ROUNDS 2 AND 3 Work even in established patterns.

ROUND 4 Knit to marker, M1, slip marker, K1, slip marker, M1, knit to end of Needle 2, work 41 stitches in Diamond Pattern Stitch.

ROUNDS 5 AND 6 Work even in established patterns.

ROUNDS 7–34 Repeat Rounds 4–6 nine more times, then work Round 4 once more. *You now have* 97 stitches total, 56 stitches on Needles 1 and 2 and 41 stitches on Needles 3 and 4.

NEXT ROUND Work even in established patterns.

NOTE You may find it easier to use short lengths of yarn as string holders when placing stitches on hold for the thumb and fingers.

NEXT ROUND K31, place next 25 thumb stitches on string holder, cast on 1 stitch, rejoin for working in the round, work 41 stitches in Diamond Pattern Stitch. *You now have* 73 stitches. Redistribute stitches, if necessary, so there are 16 stitches each on Needles 1 and 2.

NEXT 6 ROUNDS Work even in established patterns until mitten measures about 4" (10 cm) from top of ribbing.

Dividing for Flap

SET UP K32 Palm stitches and place on string holder. Work 41 stitches in Diamond Pattern Stitch and, with stitches still on the needles, run a smooth string of contrasting color through these stitches to mark this row for picking up stitches later. Cast on 32 new stitches for Palm side of Flap and join into round. Round starts at beginning of Back stitches.

ROUNDS 1–6 Work 41 Back stitches in Diamond Pattern Stitch, *K1, P1; repeat from * to end of round.

NEXT ROUND Work 41 stitches in Diamond Pattern Stitch, knit to end of round.

NEXT ROUNDS Repeat the last round until piece measures 5" (12.5 cm) from top of cuff ribbing and about 1" (2.5 cm) from top of Flap ribbing, ending on Diamond Pattern Stitch Round 5.

Decreasing for Top

SET UP Redistribute stitches for Back (Needles 1 and 2) and Palm (Needles 3 and 4) as follows.

Needle 1: 18 stitches

Needle 2: 19 stitches

Needles 3 and 4: 18 stitches on each needle

ROUND 1 Ssk, work in Diamond Pattern Stitch to last 2 stitches of Needle 2, K2tog, ssk, knit to last 2 stitches of Needle 4, K2tog — you have decreased 4 stitches.

ROUND 2 Work in established patterns to end of round.

ROUNDS 3–20 Repeat Rounds 1 and 2 nine more times. *You now have* 33 stitches.

ROUNDS 21–23 Repeat Round 1 three times. *You now have* 21 stitches.

Place 11 Back stitches on one needle and 10 Palm stitches on another, then use Kitchener Stitch (see Techniques, page 179) to graft together the ends, working the two center stitches of the Back together as one.

Knitting the Fingers

Note: See No Holes, page 76, for picking up stitches at the base of Fingers and Thumb.

SET UP From string holder, place 32 Palm stitches on needle. With new yarn at end of Palm stitches, pick up and knit 41 stitches along the marked Back row. *You now have* 73 stitches. Redistribute stitches for Palm (Needles 1 and 2) and Back (Needles 3 and 4) as follows.

Needles 1 and 2: 18 stitches on each needle

Needle 3: 18 stitches

Needle 4: 19 stitches

ROUNDS 1–6 Knit to the end of each round.

Knitting the Little Finger

SET UP Place on two needles the first 8 stitches of round from Palm and the last 9 stitches of round from Back. Place the remaining 56 stitches on a holder. Rejoin yarn to end of Palm stitches, and to a third needle cast on 4 stitches. *You now have* 21 stitches for the little finger. Distribute the stitches as evenly as possible on four needles and join into a round.

Knit to end of each round until piece measures 1" (2.5 cm), decreasing 1 stitch in the last round. *You now have* 20 stitches.

NEXT 2 ROUNDS *K1, P1; repeat from * to end of round.

Bind off in rib.

Place remaining 56 stitches on needles. With new yarn at end of Back stitches, pick up and knit 4 stitches from cast-on stitches of Little Finger and join into a round. *You now have* 60 stitches. Round begins in the center of the 4 stitches cast on for the Little Finger.

NEXT 6 ROUNDS Knit to the end of each round.

Knitting the Ring Finger

SET UP K11 Palm stitches, cast on 4 stitches, place next 39 stitches on a holder, K10 Back stitches, and join into round. *You now have* 25 stitches. Distribute the stitches as evenly as possible on four needles and join into a round.

NEXT ROUNDS Knit to the end of each round until piece measures 1" (2.5 cm), decreasing 1 stitch in the last round. *You now have* 24 stitches.

NEXT 2 ROUNDS *K1, P1; repeat from * to end of round.

Bind off in rib.

Knitting the Middle Finger

SET UP Place on needle 8 Palm stitches closest to ring finger, cast on 4 stitches with new yarn, place on needle 9 Back stitches closest to ring finger, K9 Back stitches, pick up and knit 4 stitches from cast-on stitches of ring finger, and join into round. *You now have* 25 stitches.

NEXT ROUNDS Knit to the end of each round until piece measures 1.25" (3 cm), decreasing 1 stitch in the last round. *You now have* 24 stitches.

NEXT 2 ROUNDS *K1, P1; repeat from * to end of round.

Bind off in rib.

Knitting the Index Finger

SET UP Place remaining 22 stitches on a needle. With new yarn at end of Back stitches, pick up and knit 4 stitches from cast-on stitches of Middle Finger and join into a round. *You now have* 26 stitches.

NEXT ROUNDS Knit to the end of each round until piece measures 1" (2.5 cm).

NEXT 2 ROUNDS *K1, P1; repeat from * to end of round.

Bind off in rib.

Knitting the Thumb

SET UP Place the 25 Thumb stitches on a needle. With new yarn at end of Thumb stitches, pick up and knit 1 stitch in the corner before the single stitch cast on over Thumb gap for the hand, pick up and knit 2 stitches from the base of the cast-on stitch, then pick up and knit 1 stitch in the corner after the single cast-on stitch, and join into a round. *You now have* 29 stitches. Redistribute stitches on three needles as follows.

Needles 1 and 2: 10 stitches on each needle

Needle 3: 9 stitches

NEXT ROUNDS Knit to the end of each round until piece measures 1" (2.5 cm).

NEXT ROUND *Ssk, knit to end of needle; repeat from * two more times — you have decreased 3 stitches.

NEXT 6 ROUNDS Repeat the last round six more times. *You now have* 8 stitches.

Cut working yarn, leaving a 10" (25 cm) tail, and thread tail into a tapestry needle. Pull needle through all remaining stitches, drawstring-fashion, then pass through these stitches once again, draw up tight, and fasten off to close top of thumb. Weave in the end.

Right Mitten

Work as for Left Mitten until you have completed 2.5" (6.5 cm) of rib and the first round after the rib. *You now have* 73 stitches.

Knitting the Hand

SET UP Redistribute stitches for Back (Needles 1 and 2) and Palm (Needles 3 and 4) as follows.

Needle 1: 20 stitches

Needle 2: 21 stitches

Needles 3 and 4: 16 stitches on each needle

NOTE Throughout this section, work 41 Back stitches on Needles 1 and 2 in Diamond Pattern Stitch and 32 Palm stitches on Needles 3 and 4 in Stockinette Stitch.

ROUND 1 (FIRST INCREASE ROUND FOR THUMB) Work 41 stitches in Diamond Pattern Stitch, M1, place marker, K1 (center Thumb stitch), place marker, M1, K31.

ROUNDS 2 AND 3 Work even in established patterns.

ROUND 4 Work 41 stitches in Diamond Pattern Stitch, knit to marker, M1, slip marker, K1, slip marker, M1, knit to end of round.

ROUNDS 5 AND 6 Work even in established patterns.

ROUNDS 7–34 Repeat Rounds 4–6 nine more times, then work Round 4 once more. *You now have* 97 stitches total: 41 stitches on Needles 1 and 2 and 56 stitches on Needles 3 and 4.

NEXT ROUND Work even in established patterns.

NEXT ROUND Work 41 stitches in Diamond Pattern Stitch, place next 25 Thumb stitches on string holder, cast on 1 stitch, K31, and rejoin for working in the round. *You now have* 73 stitches. Redistribute stitches, if necessary, so there are 16 stitches each on Needles 3 and 4.

NEXT 6 ROUNDS Work even in established patterns until mitten measures about 4" (10 cm) from top of ribbing.

Dividing for Flap

SET UP Work 41 stitches in Diamond Pattern Stitch and, with stitches still on the needles, run a smooth string of contrasting color through these stitches to mark this row for picking up stitches later. Place 32 Palm stitches on string holder. Cast on 32 new stitches for Palm side of Flap and join into round. Round starts at beginning of Back stitches.

Complete Flap ribbing, Stockinette Stitch, and decrease sections as for Left Mitten.

Knitting the Fingers

SET UP Place on needle 32 Palm stitches from string holder. With new yarn at end of Palm stitches, pick up and knit 41 stitches along the marked Back row. *You now have* 73 stitches.

Redistribute stitches for Palm (Needles 1 and 2) and Back (Needles 3 and 4) as follows.

Needles 1 and 2: 18 stitches on each needle

Needle 3: 18 stitches

Needle 4: 19 stitches

ROUNDS 1–6 Knit to the end of each round.

Knitting the Little Finger

SET UP Place first 28 Palm stitches on a holder, K8 Palm stitches, K9 Back stitches, place remaining 28 Back stitches on a holder, cast on 4 stitches. *You now have* 21 stitches for Little Finger.

Complete as for Left Mitten Little Finger

Place remaining 56 stitches on a needle. With new yarn at end of Palm stitches, pick up and knit 4 stitches from cast-on stitches of Little Finger and join into round. *You now have* 60 stitches. Round begins in the center of the 4 stitches cast on for Little Finger.

NEXT 6 ROUNDS Knit to the end of each round.

Knitting the Ring Finger

SET UP K10 Back stitches, place remaining 20 Back stitches on a holder, cast on 4 stitches, place first 19 Palm stitches on a holder, K11 Palm stitches, and join into a round. *You now have* 25 stitches.

Complete as for Left Mitten Ring Finger.

Knitting the Middle Finger

SET UP Place on a needle 8 Palm stitches closest to ring finger. With new yarn, pick up and knit 4 stitches from cast-on for ring finger, place on needle 9 Back stitches closest to ring finger, K9 Back stitches, cast on 4 stitches, and join into round. *You now have* 25 stitches.

Complete as for Left Mitten Middle Finger.

Knitting the Index Finger

SET UP Place remaining 22 stitches on a needle. With new yarn at end of Palm stitches, pick up and knit 4 stitches from cast-on stitches of Middle Finger and join into a round. *You now have* 26 stitches.

Complete as for Left Mitten Index Finger.

Knitting the Thumb

Work as for Left Mitten Thumb.

Finishing

Weave in all ends, using tails to close up any holes that have formed at the base of fingers or thumb despite your best efforts. Wash and block.

[I Met His Friends] Vest

WHEN YOUR BOYFRIEND wants to introduce you to his friends, you know you're special. Of course, it's notable when he agrees to meet *your* friends, but it's extraordinary when it goes the other way. Let's hope you like them — remember, these are the folks who could be taking up your sofa space and breathing your air for years to come. After thinking long and hard about his cohorts, if you still want to move ahead, it may be time to make him a full-size garment. This simple-to-knit vest is a good place to start.

It uses needles in only one size, has minimal shaping, and requires no finishing beyond joining the seams and weaving in the ends. The vest's pattern, comprising a Pattern Stitch (Body Stitch) of three rows of Stockinette Stitch and one row of K1, P1 rib, is very easy to see, making it a snap to count the repeats so you can be sure of having the same number of rows on the front and the back of the vest.

YARN
Louet Sales Gems Topaz, 100% merino
  wool, 168 yd (154 m) per 100 g
Yarn band gauge: 4.5 to 5 stitches = 1"
  (2.5 cm) on US 5 to 7 (3.75 to 4.5 mm)
  needles
Color: 02 Tobacco, 5, 6, 6 skeins,
  depending on size

FINISHED SIZE
42", 46", 50" (106.5, 117, 127 cm) chest.
  Model shown is size 46" (117 cm).

GAUGE
22 stitches and 30 rows = 4" (10 cm)
  in Pattern Stitch (Body Stitch)

NEEDLES
US 7 (4.5 mm) *or size you need to obtain
  the correct gauge*

NOTIONS
Markers, string or scrap yarn for stitch
  holders, tapestry needle

Rib Stitch

(Even Number of Stitches)

ROW 1 (RIGHT SIDE) K2, *P1, K1; repeat from * to end of row.

ROW 2 (WRONG SIDE) *P1, K1; repeat from * to last 2 stitches, P2.

Repeat Rows 1 and 2 for pattern.

Knitting the Back

Ribbing

	Small	Medium	Large
SET UP Cast on	116 sts	126 sts	138 sts

NOTES Consider using the 1/1 Rib Cast-On (see Techniques, page 175). Also see Two-Knit Rib on page 107.

ROWS 1 AND 2 Work in Rib Stitch.

	Small	Medium	Large
NEXT ROWS Continue in Rib Stitch, ending with a wrong-side row, until piece measures	2.5" (6.5 cm)	2.5" (6.5 cm)	3" (7.5 cm)

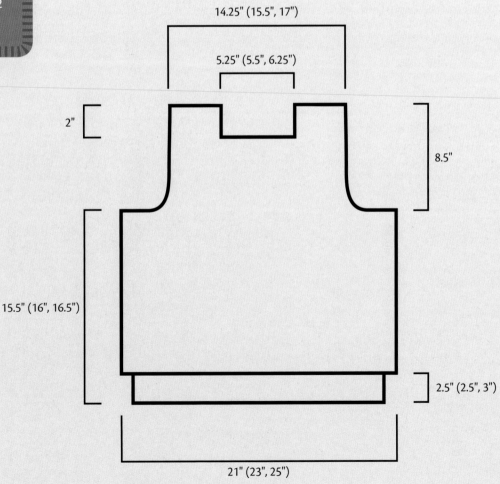

14.25" (15.5", 17")

5.25" (5.5", 6.25")

2"

8.5"

15.5" (16", 16.5")

2.5" (2.5", 3")

21" (23", 25")

pattern stitch

Body Stitch

(Even Number of Stitches)

ROW 1 (RIGHT SIDE) Knit.

ROW 2 (WRONG SIDE) Purl.

ROW 3 Knit.

ROW 4 P1 (edge stitch), *K1, P1; repeat from * to last stitch, P1 (edge stitch).

Repeat Rows 1–4 for pattern.

Body

ROWS 1–4 Work in Body Stitch.

NEXT ROWS Continue in Body Stitch, ending with Row 4 of pattern, until piece measures from cast-on edge	14.5" (37 cm)	15" (38 cm)	15.5" (39.5 cm)

Armhole Ribbing

NOTE In this section, work bands of K1, P1 rib along each underarm edge for approximately 1" (2.5 cm) before binding off to provide the armholes with a knit-as-you-go edging — no stitches to pick up later! The K1, P1 rib continues along the vertical armhole edges to create a self-finish for the armholes.

ROW 1 K1 (edge stitch), *K1, P1; repeat from * over next	18 sts	20 sts	22 sts

Work established Body Stitch to last	18 sts	20 sts	22 sts
*P1, K1; repeat from * to the end of the row. *You now have* at the beginning of right-side rows and in K1, P1 rib (including edge stitch)	19 sts	21sts	23 sts
and at the end of right-side rows in P1, K1, rib	18 sts	20 sts	22 sts

Note: Row ends K1.

NEXT ROWS Maintain Body Stitch and K1, P1 rib as established, ending with Row 4 of Body Stitch, until piece measures from cast-on edge approximately	15.5" (39.5 cm)	16" (40.5 cm)	16.5" (42 cm)

Armhole Bind-Off

NOTE In order to keep the pattern symmetrical, with a knit stitch in the body at each side where the K1, P1 ribbed armhole edging meets the body, bind off one stitch more at the left underarm than at the right underarm.

ROW 1 (RIGHT SIDE) Bind off in ribbing	13 sts	15 sts	17 sts

You now have 1 knit stitch on the right needle for armhole ribbing.

*P1, K1; repeat from * once more, P1. *You now have* 6 stitches on the right needle for armhole ribbing.

Work Body Stitch and K1, P1 rib as established to end of row.

ROW 2 Bind off in ribbing	12 sts	14 sts	16 sts

You now have 1 purl stitch on the right needle.

*K1, P1; repeat from * once more, K1. *You now have* 6 stitches on the right needle for armhole ribbing.

Work in Body Stitch to last 6 stitches, then work in established rib pattern to end. *You now have*	91 sts	97 sts	105 sts
These are arranged at center as Body Stitch:	79 sts	85 sts	93 sts

plus 6 stitches at each side in K1, P1 rib for all sizes.

ROWS 3 AND 4 Work to end of each row in established pattern, ending with Row 4 of Body Stitch.

Armhole Decreases

ROW 1 *K1, P1; repeat from * two more times, ssk, work Body Stitch as established to last 8 stitches, K2tog, *P1, K1; repeat from * two more times. You have just decreased a total of 2 stitches.

ROWS 2–4 Work 3 rows in established patterns.

ROWS 5–24 Repeat Rows 1–4 five more times. *You now have*	79 sts	85 sts	93 sts

NEXT ROWS Work in established patterns, ending with Row 4 of Body Stitch, until piece measures from cast-on edge	23" (58.5 cm)	23.5" (59.5 cm)	24" (61 cm)

Neck Ribbing

Temporarily mark with scrap yarn or removable markers the center	41 sts	43 sts	47 sts

ROW 1 Work in established patterns to marked stitches.

Work center back neck stitches as *P1, K1; repeat from * and then P1.	20 times	21 times	23 times

Work in established patterns to end of row.

ROWS 2–4 Work patterns as established in Row 1, maintaining center-back neck stitches in new rib pattern and ending with Row 4 of Body Stitch. Piece now measures from cast-on edge	24" (61 cm)	24.5" (62 cm)	25" (63.5 cm)

Place on holder	79 sts	85 sts	93 sts

Knitting the Front

Work as for Back, ending with Row 4 of Body Stitch, until piece measures	21" (53.5 cm)	21.5" (54.5 cm)	22" (56 cm)

Neck Ribbing

Temporarily mark with scrap yarn or removable markers the center	41 sts	43 sts	47 sts

ROW 1 Work in established patterns to marked stitches.

Work center-front neck stitches as *P1, K1; repeat from *	20 times	21 times	23 times

and then P1.

Work in established patterns to end of row.

ROWS 2–4 Work patterns as established in Row 1, maintaining center-back neck stitches in new rib pattern and ending with Row 4 of Body Stitch. Piece now measures	22" (56 cm)	22.5" (57 cm)	23" (58.5 cm)

ROW 5 Work in established patterns the first	25 sts	27 sts	29 sts

Place the stitches you just worked on a holder for Left Front.

Bind off in established patterns for center-front neck	29 sts	31 sts	35 sts

NOTE The stitch remaining on the needle after binding off the stitches at center front becomes the first K1 for the rib pattern at neck edge of Right Front.

Work in established patterns to end of row.

On the needle for Right Front *you now have*	25 sts	27 sts	29 sts

NEXT ROWS Working Right Front stitches only, continue in established patterns, with 6 stitches in ribbing at each end of needle, until piece measures about ¼ inch (0.6 cm) less than Back from cast-on edge, ending on Row 2 of Body Stitch. Place Right Front stitches on holder.

Return Left Front stitches to the needle. With wrong side facing you, attach yarn at neck edge and work in established patterns as for Right Front until piece measures the same as Right Front, ending with Row 2 of Body Stitch.

Finishing

Using Three-Needle Bind-Off or Variation (see Techniques, page 177), join Left Front and Back shoulders	25 sts	27 sts	29 sts
Bind off center neck stitches in Body Stitch	29 sts	31 sts	35 sts
Return Right Front stitches to needle and join Right Front and Back shoulders	25 sts	27 sts	29 sts

Sew side seams, weave in all ends, then wash and block.

Two-Knit-Rib Start

The I Met His Friends Vest and other patterns in the book start by casting on an even number of stitches for K1, P1 ribbing, but the instructions begin with K2. The first and last Stockinette Stitches of each row are edge stitches designed to disappear into the seam when the garment or item is sewn together. The rib that shows on the right side of both front and back begins with a knit and ends with a purl, and the pattern continues uninterrupted across the seam once it is sewn.

[He Met My Parents]
HOUNDSTOOTH Vest

IF YOUR RELATIONSHIP HAS PROGRESSED to the point of family introductions and he's met your folks, you're ready for the next knitting challenge. It's still too early for sleeves, but a two-color vest that requires finishing for the neck and armholes will provide plenty of knitting stimulation.

This vest is worked in a subtle, two-tone houndstooth pattern. The darker color is used for ribbing and edging around the V-neck and armholes. When knitting with two colors, carry the yarns loosely across the back to prevent puckering. Note that working with two colors pulls in the knitting somewhat and creates a denser fabric with more stitches per inch than you'd find in knitting that uses only one color.

YARN
Jaeger Matchmaker Merino
Double Knitting, 100% merino
wool, 130 yd (120 m) per 50 g
Yarn band gauge: 22 stitches =
4" (10 cm) on US 6 (4 mm)
needles
Color A = 698 Indigo (navy), 5, 5,
6 skeins, depending on size
Color B = 856 Buddleia (purple),
4, 4, 5 skeins

FINISHED SIZE
39", 42", 45" (99, 106.5, 114.5 cm)
chest. Model shown is size 39"
(99 cm).

GAUGE
28 stitches and 29 rows = 4"
(10 cm) in Pattern Stitch
(Houndstooth Check Stitch)
on larger needle

NEEDLES
US 4 (3.5 mm) and 6 (4 mm)
straight needles and one US
5 (3.75 mm) circular needle,
16" (40.5 cm) long, *or sizes you
need to obtain the correct gauge*

NOTIONS
Tapestry needle, stitch holders

ABBREVIATIONS
CA = Color A
CB = Color B
M1= make 1 increase
(see Techniques, page 181)

Knitting the Back

Ribbing

SET UP Cast on with CA and smaller needles	Small	Medium	Large
	138 sts	146 sts	158 sts

NOTES Consider using 1/1 Rib Cast-On (see Techniques, page 175). Also, see Two-Knit-Rib Start on page 107.

ROWS 1 AND 2 Work in Rib Stitch.

NEXT ROWS Continue in Rib Stitch, ending with a wrong-side row, until piece measures 2" (5 cm).

Body

Change to larger needles.

ROWS 1–4 Join CB and work in Houndstooth Check Stitch. (See Two-Color Stranding, page 115.)

NEXT ROWS Continue in Houndstooth Check Stitch until piece measures 13.5" (34.5 cm) from cast-on edge for all sizes, ending with Row 4 of pattern.

Armhole Bind-Off

	Small	Medium	Large
At the beginning of the next two rows, bind off	7 sts	9 sts	13 sts
You now have	124 sts	128 sts	132 sts

Armhole Decreases

NOTE Continue to work 1 edge stitch at each side in CA throughout and center stitches in established Houndstooth Check Stitch.

ROW 1 K1 CA, ssk in color required to maintain pattern, work in Houndstooth Check Stitch to last 3 stitches, K2tog in color required to maintain pattern, K1 CA. You have just decreased 2 stitches.

ROW 2 P1 CA, work in Houndstooth Check Stitch to last stitch, P1 CA.

	Small	Medium	Large
NEXT ROWS Repeat these two rows	12 more times	13 more times	14 more times
You now have	98 sts	100 sts	102 sts

pattern stitch

Rib Stitch

(Even Number of Stitches)

ROW 1 (RIGHT SIDE) K2, *P1, K1; repeat from * to end of row.

ROW 2 (WRONG SIDE) *P1, K1; repeat from * to last 2 stitches, P2.

Repeat Rows 1 and 2 for pattern.

pattern stitch

Houndstooth Check Stitch

(Multiples of 4 Stitches Plus 1 Edge Stitch at Each Side)

ROW 1 K1 CA (edge stitch), K1 CA, *K1 CB, K3 CA; repeat from * to last 4 stitches, K1 CB, K2 CA, K1 CA (edge stitch).

ROW 2 P1 CA (edge stitch), *P3 CB, P1 CA; repeat from * to last stitch, P1 CA (edge stitch).

ROW 3 K1 CA (edge stitch), *K3 CB, K1 CA; repeat from * to last stitch, K1 CA (edge stitch).

ROW 4 P1 CA (edge stitch), P1 CA, *P1 CB, P3 CA; repeat from * to last 4 stitches, P1 CB, P2 CA, P1 CA (edge stitch).

Repeat Rows 1–4 for pattern.

Work in Houndstooth Check Stitch and edge stitches in CA as established until piece measures from cast-on edge	23.5" (59.5 cm)	24" (61 cm)	24.5" (62 cm)

ending on Row 3 of Houndstooth Check Pattern.

Place 27 stitches at each side on separate holders for shoulders, and place on another holder for back neck	44 sts	46 sts	48 sts

Knitting the Front

Work as for back until you have completed armhole decreases, ending with Row 4 of Houndstooth Check Stitch. *You now have*	98 sts	100 sts	102 sts
From bind-off rows, armholes measure approximately	4" (10 cm)	4" (10 cm)	4.5" (11.5 cm)

Neck Shaping for Left Front

ROW 1 (RIGHT SIDE) K1 CA, K (in established color pattern)	45 sts	46 sts	47 sts

K2tog in color required for pattern, K1 CA. Place on holder for Right Front remaining	49 sts	50 sts	51 sts

ROW 2 P1 CA, work in established pattern to last stitch, P1 CA.

ROW 3 K1 CA, work in established pattern to last 3 stitches, K2tog, K1 CA.

ROW 4 P1 CA, work in established pattern to last stitch, P1 CA.

NEXT ROWS Repeat Rows 3 and 4	20 more times	21 more times	22 more times

You now have 27 stitches for all sizes. Work even, if necessary, until Left Front measures same as Back, ending with Row 2 of Houndstooth Check Stitch. Place stitches on holder for shoulder.

Neck Shaping for Right Front

Return to larger needle from holder	49 sts	50 sts	51 sts

Rejoin yarns with right side of piece facing you, ready to work a right-side row.

ROW 1 K1 CA, ssk in color required for pattern, work in established pattern to last stitch, K1 CA.

ROW 2 P1 CA, work in established pattern to last stitch, P1 CA.

NEXT ROWS Repeat Rows 1 and 2	21 more times	22 more times	23 more times

You now have 27 stitches for all sizes. Work even, if necessary, until Right Front measures the same as Back and Left Front, ending with Row 2 of Houndstooth Check Stitch.

Using Three-Needle Bind-Off or Variation (see Techniques, pages 177–178), join 27 stitches of Right Front and Back at right shoulder. Return Left Front stitches to needle and join Left Front and Back shoulders.

Neck Ribbing

NOTE Neck ribbing is worked in the round in K1, P1 rib using the circular needle. In order to create a decorative decrease at the center-front V, the center-front stitch must be a knit stitch.

SET UP With circular needle and CA, begin at neck edge of left shoulder seam. Pick up and knit along shaped Left Front neck edge

Pick up and knit along shaped Left Front neck edge	38 sts	40 sts	42 sts

Work an M1 increase in the middle of the 2 stitches at center front, where the piece divides for the V-neck, and mark this stitch with a removable marker, length of yarn, or safety pin attached to the stitch itself (do not place markers on the needle).

Pick up and knit along shaped right-front edge	37 sts	39 sts	41 sts
Return to needle from back neck holder and knit	44 sts	46 sts	48 sts
You now have	120 sts	126 sts	132 sts

Join into a round and place marker at beginning of round.

ROUND 1 Begin working K1, P1 rib as follows: *K1, P1; repeat from * to marked stitch at center front, K1 (center stitch), **P1, K1; repeat from ** to last stitch, ending with P1.

ROUND 2 Work in established rib to 1 stitch before marked center stitch, slip 2 stitches as if to K2tog, P1, pass 2 slipped stitches over, work in established rib to end of round. You have just decreased 2 stitches.

ROUND 3 Work in established rib to marked center stitch, K1 (center stitch), work in established rib to end of round.

NEXT ROUNDS Repeat Rounds 2 and 3 once, then work Round 2 one more time. You have just completed 6 rounds in rib. *You now have*	114 sts	120 sts	126 sts

Bind off all stitches in rib pattern.

Armhole Ribbing

Sew side seams. Beginning at side seam, with circular needle pick up and knit around each armhole	140 sts	150 sts	160 sts

Join into a round and place marker for beginning of round.

ROUND 1 Begin working K1, P1 ribbing as follows: *K1, P1; repeat from * to end of round.

NEXT ROUNDS Repeat Round 1 five more times. You have just completed 6 rounds in rib.

Bind off all stitches in rib pattern.

Finishing

Weave in all ends, then wash and block.

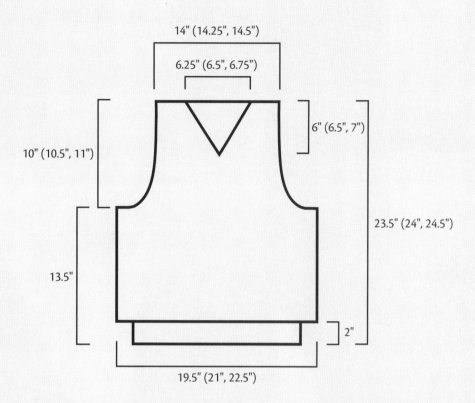

14" (14.25", 14.5")

6.25" (6.5", 6.75")

6" (6.5", 7")

10" (10.5", 11")

23.5" (24", 24.5")

13.5"

2"

19.5" (21", 22.5")

Two-Color Stranding

When changing color on a right-side row, bring the new color (the light yarn in the illustration) *over* the old color (the dark yarn) and knit the stitch (fig. 1). Keep the stitches stretched out on the needle so that the float on the back is long enough to span the stitches in the old color without puckering.

When changing color on a wrong-side row, drop the old color (the dark yarn in the illustration), pick up the new color (the light yarn), and purl the stitch (fig. 2). Again, keep the stitches stretched out to prevent puckering.

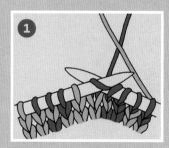

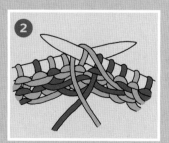

[I Met His Parents]
ZIPPY DIAMOND Vest

IF YOUR BOYFRIEND IS LIKE MANY OTHER MALES, it's a big deal for him to bring you home to meet the folks. Although many men could handle meeting your friends and family without too much thought about where the relationship is headed, bringing you home to meet his family is a milestone: It means he's serious, and may well deserve this labor of love.

This vest is worked back and forth as one piece to the armholes, then it's divided so that the back and front are worked separately. The simple rolled Stockinette edging is created by picking up stitches around the armholes and front opening. Begin with an odd number of stitches so the bottom rib will be symmetrical on either side of center front, then decrease to an even number of stitches for working the pattern.

YARN

Classic Elite Renaissance, 100% wool,
110 yd (100 m) per 50 g
Yarn band gauge: 4.5 to 5 stitches = 1" (2.5 cm)
on US 7 or 8 (4.5 or 5 mm) needles
Color: 7178 Tiled Roof (rust), 9, 10, 11 skeins,
depending on size

FINISHED SIZE

38", 42", 46.5" (96.5, 107, 118 cm) chest.
Model shown is size 42" (107 cm).

GAUGE

22 stitches and 28 rows = 4" (10 cm) in
Pattern Stitch (Diamond Pattern Stitch)
using larger needle

NEEDLES

US 8 (5 mm) and 6 (4 mm) circular needles, 32"
(80 cm) long; US 6 (4 mm) circular needle 16"
(40 cm) long for armhole edging; *or sizes you
need to obtain the correct gauge*

NOTIONS

Tapestry needle, stitch holders, stitch marker, cable
needle, 14" (35.5 cm) separating zipper for all
sizes, sewing needle, contrasting thread for bast-
ing zipper, matching thread for inserting zipper

ABBREVIATIONS

RT = right twist: Skip the first stitch; with the needle
in *front*, knit the second stitch and leave on
needle; knit the first stitch and slide both stitches
off needle.

LT = left twist: Skip the first stitch; with the needle
in back, knit the second stitch and leave on
needle; knit the first stitch and slide both stitches
off needle.

RPT = right purl twist: Skip the first stitch; with the
needle in *front*, knit the second stitch and leave
on needle; purl the first stitch and slide both
stitches off needle.

LPT = left purl twist: Skip the first stitch; with the
needle *in back*, purl the second stitch through
the back loop and leave on needle; knit the first
stitch and slide both stitches off needle.

Rib Stitch

pattern stitch

(Odd Number of Stitches)

ROW 1 (RIGHT SIDE) K2, *P1, K1; repeat from * to last 3 stitches, end P1, K2.

ROW 2 (WRONG SIDE) P2, *K1, P1; repeat from * to last 3 stitches, end K1, P2.

Repeat Rows 1 and 2 for pattern.

Diamond Pattern Stitch

pattern stitch

(Multiple of 12 Stitches Plus 16)

Note: Refer to chart on page 119.

ROW 1 (RIGHT SIDE) K1 (edge stitch), P1, K1, *P10, RT; repeat from * to last 13 stitches, ending with P10, K1, P1, K1.

ROWS 2–22 (WRONG SIDE) Knit the knits and purl the purls.

ROW 3 K1, P1, LPT, *P8, RPT, LPT; repeat from * to last 12 stitches, ending with P8, RPT, P1, K1.

ROW 5 K1, P2, *LPT, P6, RPT, P2; repeat from * to last stitch, ending with K1.

ROW 7 K1, P2, *P1, LPT, P4, RPT, P3; repeat from * to last stitch, ending with K1.

ROW 9 K1, P2, *P2, LPT, P2, RPT, P4; repeat from * to last stitch, ending with K1.

ROW 11 K1, P2, *P3, LPT, RPT, P5; repeat from * to last stitch, ending with K1.

ROW 13 K1, P2, *P4, LT, P6; repeat from * to last stitch, ending with K1.

ROW 15 K1, P2, *P3, RPT, LPT, P5; repeat from * to last stitch, ending with K1.

ROW 17 K1, P2, *P2, RPT, P2, LPT, P4; repeat from * to last stitch, ending with K1.

ROW 19 K1, P2, *P1, RPT, P4, LPT, P3; repeat from * to last stitch, ending with K1.

ROW 21 K1, P2, *RPT, P6, LPT, P2; repeat from * to last stitch, ending with K1.

ROW 23 K1, P1, RPT, *P8, LPT, RPT; repeat from * to last 12 stitches, ending with P8, LPT, P1, K1.

ROW 24 Knit the knits and purl the purls.

Repeat Rows 1–24 for pattern.

Knitting the Body

Ribbing

	Small	Medium	Large
SET UP Cast on with smaller needle	209 sts	233 sts	257 sts

ROWS 1 AND 2 Work in Rib Stitch.

NEXT ROWS Continue in Rib Stitch, ending with a right-side row, until piece measures 2.5" (6.5 cm). Change to larger needle.

Body

	Small	Medium	Large
SET-UP ROW (WRONG SIDE) P1, K1, P1, *K10, P2; repeat from *	8 times	9 times	10 times
K5, K2tog, K4, P2, **K10, P2; repeat from **	7 times	8 times	9 times
K10, P1, K1, P1. *You now have*	208 sts	232 sts	256 sts

NEXT ROWS Repeat Rows 1–24 of Diamond Pattern Stitch three times, then work Rows 1–12 once more. You have just completed 84 Diamond Pattern Stitch rows in total and piece measures 14.5" (37 cm) from cast-on edge for all sizes.

- ☐ K on RS; P on WS
- ⊟ P on RS; K on WS
- ◹ RT
- ◺ LT
- ◿ RPT
- ◺ LPT

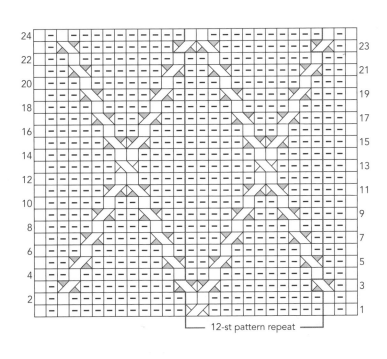

12-st pattern repeat

Divide for Back and Fronts

Continuing in established pattern, work	56 sts	62 sts	70 sts
From these stitches just worked, place on one holder for Right Front the first	44 sts	50 sts	54 sts
and on another holder for Right Armhole the last	12 sts	12 sts	16 sts
Work in established pattern for Back for the next	96 sts	108 sts	116 sts
Place on a holder for Left Front and Armhole	56 sts	62 sts	70 sts
For Back, *you now have*	96 sts	108 sts	116 sts

Back

NOTE See Decreasing in Pattern for Armholes and V-Neck on pages 126–127 for how to work decreases two stitches in from each edge of the piece while maintaining Diamond Pattern Stitch.

ROW 1 (WRONG SIDE) Work in established pattern.

NEXT ROWS (BEGINNING WITH NEXT RIGHT-SIDE ROW) Decrease 1 stitch at each end of needle every right side row	8 times	9 times	10 times
You now have	80 sts	90 sts	96 sts
NEXT ROWS Continue working in established pattern until piece measures from cast-on edge approximately	25" (63.5 cm)	25" (63.5 cm)	26.5" (67.5 cm)
End with Diamond Pattern Stitch	Row 12	Row 12	Row 24
Of the remaining stitches, place on three holders: for one shoulder the first	21 sts	24 sts	26 sts
for the back neck the next	38 sts	42 sts	44 sts
for the other shoulder the last	21 sts	24 sts	26 sts

Right Front

NOTES See Decreasing in Pattern for Armholes and V-Neck, pages 126–127, for how to work decreases two stitches in from each edge of the piece while maintaining Diamond Pattern Stitch. Armhole and V-neck shaping are worked at the same time; before you work, be sure to read through the next directions completely for correct results.

SET UP Return to larger needle for the Right Front	44 sts	50 sts	54 sts

Leave Right Armhole stitches on holder. With wrong side facing you, join yarn.

ROW 1 Work 1 wrong-side row in established pattern.

NEXT ROWS (BEGINNING WITH THE NEXT RIGHT-SIDE ROW) Work armhole shaping by decreasing 1 stitch at end of needle (armhole edge) every right-side row	8 times	9 times	10 times

At the same time, beginning with the same right-side row on which armhole shaping begins, work neck shaping by decreasing 1 stitch at beginning of needle (neck edge) *every other* right-side row	15 times	17 times	18 times

After completing all shaping, *you now have*	21 sts	24 sts	26 sts

NEXT ROWS Work even until piece measures same
length as Back, ending with a right-side row in
Diamond Pattern Stitch

	Row 11	Row 11	Row 23

Place Right Shoulder stitches on holder.

Left Front

NOTES See Decreasing in Pattern for Armholes and V-Neck, pages 126–127, for
how to work decreases two stitches in from each edge of the piece while maintaining Diamond Pattern Stitch. Armhole and V-neck shaping are worked at the
same time; before you work, please be sure to read through the next directions
completely for correct results.

SET UP Return to larger needle for the Left Front	56 sts	62 sts	70 sts

With right side facing you, join yarn. Work in established pattern for Left Armhole	12 sts	12 sts	16 sts

and place these stitches on holder.

ROWS 1–2 Work 2 rows even in established pattern, ending with a wrong-side row for Left Front	44 sts	50 sts	54 sts
NEXT ROWS (BEGINNING WITH THE NEXT RIGHT-SIDE ROW) Work armhole shaping by decreasing 1 stitch at the beginning of needle (armhole edge) every right-side row	8 times	9 times	10 times
At the same time, beginning with the same right-side row on which armhole shaping begins, work neck shaping by decreasing 1 stitch at end of needle (neck edge) *every other* right-side row	15 times	17 times	18 times
After completing all shaping, *you now have*	21 sts	24 sts	26 sts
NEXT ROWS Work even until piece measures same length as Back and Right Front, ending with a right-side row in Diamond Pattern Stitch:	Row 11	Row 11	Row 23

Place Left Shoulder stitches on holder.

Joining the Shoulders

Using Three-Needle Bind-Off Variation (see Techniques, page 178), join stitches for Right Front and Back Shoulders. In the same manner, join Left Front and Back Shoulders.

Finishing

Armhole Edging

SET UP From armhole holder, place on smaller 16" (40 cm) circular needle	12 sts	12 sts	16 sts
With right side facing, join yarn to end of these stitches. Pick up and knit around armhole edge	132 sts	132 sts	144 sts
You now have	144 sts	144 sts	160 sts

Join into a round and place marker for beginning of round.

NEXT ROUNDS Work in Stockinette Stitch for 6 rounds. Bind off loosely. Repeat for other armhole.

Front Edging

SET UP With smaller 32" (80 cm) circular needle and right side facing you, beginning at lower edge of Right Front, pick up and knit to Right Shoulder	131 sts	132 sts	139 sts
Return to needle for Back Neck	38 sts	42 sts	44 sts

Work decreases at each K2 of pattern (final twist) to prevent Back Neck from stretching, as follows:

Sizes 38" and 42"
*Knit to one stitch before K2 pair, place 2 stitches on cable needle and hold in front, K2tog (remaining stitch of K2 pair and the stitch after it), ssk the 2 stitches from cable needle; repeat from * as required, knit to end of Back Neck stitches.

Size 46.5"
*Knit to one stitch before K2 pair, place 2 stitches on cable needle and hold in back, K2tog (remaining stitch of K2 pair and the stitch after it), ssk the 2 stitches from cable needle; repeat from * as required, knit to end of Back Neck stitches.

Pick up and knit from Left Shoulder to lower edge of Right Front	131 sts	132 sts	139 sts
You now have	294 sts	300 sts	314 sts

NEXT ROWS Work in Stockinette Stitch for 9 rows. Bind off loosely.

Adding the Zipper

Baste zipper in place using sewing needle and contrasting thread, aligning lower edge of zipper with lower edge of vest and matching stitching line on zipper tape to line of picked-up stitches for front edging. Sew zipper in place with matching thread, keeping stitches as close as possible to the zipper teeth without the zipper catching in the stitches.

Making and Adding Zipper Facings (Make 2)

With larger needle, cast on 4 stitches and work in Stockinette Stitch until facing is the same length as zipper tape when slightly stretched. Bind off facing stitches. Place facing on inside of vest to cover zipper tape, but not so close that zipper will catch the facing. Sew center-front edge of facing to zipper with matching thread and sewing needle, then sew other edge of facing to wrong side of vest using project yarn and tapestry needle.

Weave in all ends. Wash and block.

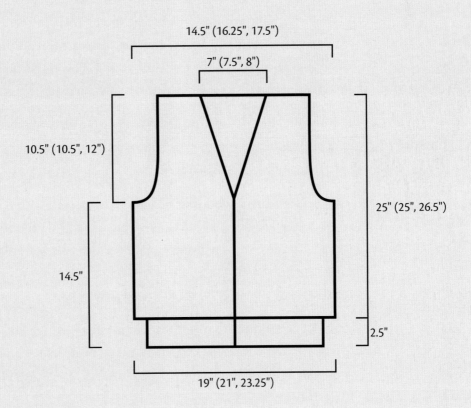

14.5" (16.25", 17.5")

7" (7.5", 8")

10.5" (10.5", 12")

25" (25", 26.5")

14.5"

2.5"

19" (21", 23.25")

Decreasing in Pattern for Armholes and V-Neck

Because the knit stitches travel across this fabric, you'll be faced with a different set of decisions about how to handle them when shaping the armholes and neck. Here are my tips for working the decreases into the pattern. If you follow them, your garment will look great.

Throughout armhole and neck shaping, maintain the two edge stitches at each end of the row: On right-side rows, these edge stitches appear as K1, P1 at beginning of the row and P1, K1 at the end of the row. On the decrease rows, work all decreases on the third and fourth stitches in from each edge. Following is a guide to decreasing while maintaining the pattern, depending on how the stitches present themselves.

Case 1. The third, fourth, and fifth stitches from each end are all purl stitches. Simply work these stitches together; no special attention is needed: K1, P1, P2tog, work in pattern to last 4 stitches, P2tog, P1, K1.

Case 2. The third and fourth stitches from each end are purls, the fifth stitch from each end is a knit, and traveling knit stitches are moving out toward the edges (see fig. 1): K1, P1, slip the next 2 purl stitches onto cable needle and hold in back, K1, P2tog from cable needle, work in pattern to last 5 stitches, slip knit stitch onto cable needle and hold in front, P2tog, K1 from cable needle, P1, K1.

Case 3. The third and fourth stitches from each end are purls, the fifth stitch from each end is a knit, and traveling knit stitches are moving in toward the center. You simply work the third and fourth stitches together; no special attention is needed: Work as for Case 1 above.

Case 4. The third stitch from each end is a purl, the fourth stitch from each end is a knit, and traveling knit stitches are moving out toward the edges (see fig. 2). Work K1, P1, K2tog, work in pattern to last 4 stitches, ssk, P1, K1.

Case 5. The third stitch from each end is a purl, the fourth stitch from each end is a knit, and traveling knit stitches are moving in toward the center (fig. 3): K1, P1, slip next purl stitch to right needle as if to purl with yarn in back, slip knit stitch onto cable needle and hold in front, return slipped purl stitch to left needle, P2tog, K1 from cable needle, work in pattern to last 5 stitches, slip next purl stitch onto cable needle and hold in back, K1, slip purl stitch from cable needle to left needle, P2tog, P1, K1.

Case 6. The third stitch from each end is a knit and traveling knit stitches are moving out toward the edges (fig. 4): K1, P1, ssk, work in pattern to last 4 stitches, K2tog, P1, K1. *Note:* The third stitch from each edge remains a knit stitch after completing this decrease row.

Case 7. The third stitch from each end is a knit and the traveling knit stitches are moving in toward the center (fig. 5): K1, P1, slip knit stitch onto cable needle and hold in front, P2tog, K1 from cable needle, work in pattern to last 5 stitches, place next 2 purl stitches on cable needle and hold in back, K1, P2tog from cable needle, P1, K1. *Note:* The third stitch from each edge remains a knit stitch after completing this decrease row.

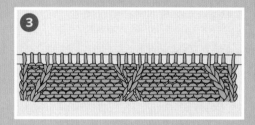

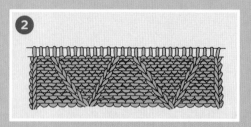

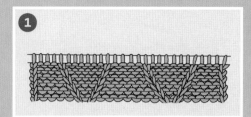

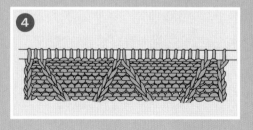

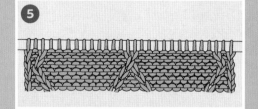

[Part-Time Living] COTTON
Classic Sweater

YOU HAVE A SPARE HAIR DRYER AT HIS PLACE and his extra toothbrush occupies a space in your bathroom. It seems there's no stopping you now, so go ahead and take the plunge: Knit him a sweater, complete with sleeves. Make this basic Stockinette Stitch crew neck in colors that flatter you — there's nothing like lounging around and reading the Sunday paper in his sweater.

This crew begins with a provisional cast-on, and the live stitches of the bottom edge are folded up and hemmed on the inside. Remember that cotton tends to have a mind of its own; it will stretch quite a bit between necessary and careful washings. It's also not a fiber to wear near water because it gets very heavy when wet. If the two of you are out boating while he wears this sweater and he falls overboard, he may have a hard time staying afloat!

YARN
Tahki Cotton Classic, 100% mercerized cotton, 108 yd (99 m) per 50 g

Yarn band gauge: 5 stitches = 1" (2.5 cm) on US 6 (4 mm) needles

Color A = 3870 Royal Blue, 11, 13, 15 skeins, depending on size

Color B = 3002 Black, 1 skein for all sizes

Color C = 3001 White, 1 skein for all sizes

FINISHED SIZE
38", 42.5", 46.5" (96.5, 108, 118 cm) chest. Model shown is size 42.5" (108 cm).

GAUGE
21 stitches and 30 rows = 4" (10 cm) in Pattern Stitch (Stockinette Stitch) on larger needles

NEEDLES
US 4 (3.5 mm) and 5 (3.75 mm) straight needles and one US 5 (3.75 mm) circular needle, 16" (40 cm) long, *or size you need to obtain the correct gauge*

NOTIONS
Tapestry needle, scrap yarn

ABBREVIATIONS
CA = Color A

CB = Color B

CC = Color C

WT = Wrap and turn (see Short Rows, pages 138–139)

M1= Make 1 increase (see Techniques, page 181)

pattern stitch

Stockinette Stitch

||||||||

ROW 1 (RIGHT SIDE) Knit.

ROW 2 (WRONG SIDE) Purl.

Repeat Rows 1 and 2 for pattern.

pattern stitch

Rib Pattern Stitch

||||||||

(Even Number of Stitches)

ROW 1 (RIGHT SIDE) K2, *P1, K1; repeat from * to end of row.

ROW 2 (WRONG SIDE) *P1, K1; repeat from * to last 2 stitches, P2.

Repeat Rows 1 and 2 for pattern.

Knitting the Back

	Small	Medium	Large
SET UP With CA, using Provisional Cast-On (see Techniques, page 176) and smaller straight needles, cast on	100 sts	112 sts	122 sts
NEXT ROWS Work in Stockinette Stitch for 1" (2.5 cm), ending with a right-side knit row.			
NEXT ROW Knit 1 wrong-side row to form a turning ridge for the hem fold line.			
Change to larger straight needles.			
NEXT ROWS Work in Stockinette Stitch, ending with a wrong-side row, until piece measures from fold line	13" (33 cm)	14" (35.5 cm)	14" (35.5 cm)
NEXT 12 ROWS Work 12 rows of stripe pattern as follows: 2 rows CB, 2 rows CA, 1 row CB, 2 rows CC, 1 row CB, 2 rows CA, 2 rows CB.			
NEXT 2 ROWS Work 2 rows even with CA.			
From fold line, piece now measures approximately	15" (38 cm)	16" (40.5 cm)	16" (40.5 cm)

Shape Armholes

	Small	Medium	Large
ROWS 1 AND 2 At the beginning of each row, bind off	4 sts	4 sts	6 sts
You now have	92 sts	104 sts	110 sts
NEXT ROWS Decrease 1 stitch at each end of needle every right-side row	6 times	6 times	7 times
You now have	80 sts	92 sts	96 sts
NEXT ROWS Continue even in Stockinette Stitch, ending with a wrong-side row, until armholes measure	8.5" (21.5 cm)	9" (23 cm)	9.5" (24 cm)

Shape Shoulders with Short Rows

NOTE See Short Rows, pages 138–139.

ROW 1 (RIGHT SIDE) Knit Wrap next stitch and turn work (WT).	72 sts	82 sts	86 sts
ROW 2 (WRONG SIDE) Purl then WT. *You now have* unworked at each end of row	64 sts 8 sts	72 sts 10 sts	76 sts 10 sts
ROW 3 Knit then WT.	56 sts	62 sts	66 sts
ROW 4 Purl then WT. *You now have* unworked at each end of row	48 sts 16 sts	52 sts 20 sts	56 sts 20 sts
ROW 5 Knit then WT.	39 sts	43 sts	46 sts
ROW 6 Purl then WT. *You now have* unworked at each end of row	30 sts 25 sts	34 sts 29 sts	36 sts 30 sts

ROW 7 Knit to end of row, working all wrapped stitches together with their wraps as you come to them.

ROW 8 Purl to end of row, working remaining wrapped stitches together with their wraps as you come to them.

Place at each end of row on separate lengths of yarn for Shoulders	25 sts	29 sts	30 sts
Place at center on another length of yarn for center Back Neck	30 sts	34 sts	36 sts

Knitting the Front

	6" (15 cm)	6.5" (16.5 cm)	7" (18 cm)
Work as for Back, ending with a wrong-side row, until armholes measure			
You now have	80 sts	92 sts	96 sts
With right side facing you, on a length of yarn for Right Front, place the last	35 sts	40 sts	41 sts
On another length of yarn place at center	10 sts	12 sts	14 sts
You now have on needle for Left Front	35 sts	40 sts	41 sts

Shape Left-Front Neck with Short Rows

	6" (15 cm)	6.5" (16.5 cm)	7" (18 cm)
ROW 1 (RIGHT SIDE) Knit then WT.	33 sts	37 sts	38 sts
ROWS 2–8 (WRONG SIDE) Purl to end of row.			
ROW 3 Knit then WT.	31 sts	35 sts	36 sts
ROW 5 Knit then WT.	29 sts	33 sts	34 sts
ROW 7 Knit then WT.	27 sts	31 sts	32 sts
ROW 9 Knit	25 sts	29 sts	30 sts
then WT. *You now have* unworked at neck edge	10 sts	11 sts	11 sts
ROW 10 Purl to end of row.			
On a length of yarn from short row section, place	10 sts	11 sts	11 sts
You now have on needle	25 sts	29 sts	30 sts

NEXT ROWS Work even in Stockinette Stitch until Left Front has five rows fewer than Back to beginning of shoulder shaping, ending with a right-side row.

Shape Left Shoulder with Short Rows

ROW 1 (WRONG SIDE) Purl	17 sts	19 sts	20 sts
then WT.			
ROWS 2 AND 4 (WRONG SIDE) Knit to end of row.			
ROW 3 Purl	9 sts	9 sts	10 sts
then WT.			
ROW 5 Purl to end of row, working all wrapped stitches together with their wraps as you come to them. On a length of yarn for Left Shoulder, place	25 sts	29 sts	30 sts

Keep ball of CA attached to these stitches to use later for joining Shoulder and finishing Neck.

Shape Right-Front Neck with Short Rows

Return to needle for Right Front	35 sts	40 sts	41 sts
With right side facing you, ready to work a right-side row, join a new ball of CA.			
ROW 1 (RIGHT SIDE) Knit to end of row.			
ROW 2 (WRONG SIDE) Purl	33 sts	37 sts	38 sts
then WT.			
ROWS 3–9 (RIGHT SIDE) Knit to end of row.			
ROW 4 Purl	31 sts	35 sts	36 sts
then WT.			
ROW 6 Purl	29 sts	33 sts	34 sts
then WT.			
ROW 8 Purl	27 sts	31 sts	32 sts
then WT.			
ROW 10 Purl	25 sts	29 sts	30 sts
then WT. *You now have* unworked at neck edge	10 sts	11 sts	11 sts

ROW 11 Knit to end of row.

On a length of yarn from short row section, place	10 sts	11 sts	11 sts
You now have on needle	25 sts	29 sts	30 sts

NEXT ROWS Work even in Stockinette Stitch until Right Front has six rows fewer than Back to beginning of shoulder shaping, ending with a wrong-side row.

Shape Right Shoulder with Short Rows

ROW 1 (RIGHT SIDE) Knit	17 sts	19 sts	20 sts
then WT.			

ROWS 2 AND 4 (WRONG SIDE) Purl to end of row.

ROW 3 Knit	9 sts	9 sts	10 sts
then WT.			

ROW 5 Knit to end of row, working all wrapped stitches together with their wraps as you come to them.

On a length of yarn for Right Shoulder, place	25 sts	29 sts	30 sts

Joining the Shoulders

Using the Three-Needle Bind-Off or Variation (see Techniques, pages 177–178), join Right Front and Back Shoulders stitches. Place last stitch of bind-off on a length of yarn. Using attached working yarn, join Left Front and Back Shoulders in the same manner, and place last stitch on a separate length of yarn.

Working the Neck Band

SET UP Place on 16" (40 cm) circular needle:

From Left Front short rows	10 sts	11 sts	11 sts
From center-front holder	10 sts	12 sts	14 sts
From Right Front short rows	10 sts	11 sts	11 sts
From Right Shoulder join	1 st	1 st	1 st
From Back-Neck holder	30 sts	34 sts	36 sts
From Left Shoulder join	1 st	1 st	1 st
You now have	62 sts	70 sts	74 sts

ROUND 1 Join CA with right side facing you to Left Shoulder join. Pick up and knit along sleeve edge of Left Front Neck

8 sts	8 sts	9 sts

Knit stitches of the Left Front short row section, working each wrapped stitch together with its wrap as you come to it and working an M1 increase after each of the 5 wrapped stitches.

Knit center

10 sts	12 sts	14 sts

Knit stitches of the Right Front short row section, working each wrapped stitch together with its wrap as you come to it and working an M1 increase after each of the 5 wrapped stitches.

Pick up and knit along selvedge of Right Front Neck

8 sts	8 sts	9 sts

Knit 1 stitch from Right Shoulder join.

Knit from Back Neck holder

30 sts	34 sts	36 sts

Knit 1 stitch from Left Shoulder join.
You now have

88 sts	96 sts	102 sts

Join into a round and place marker for beginning of round.

ROUND 2 *K1, P1; repeat from * to end of round.

NEXT ROUNDS Repeat Round 2 until Neck Band measures 1" (2.5 cm) from pickup round. Bind off loosely in rib using larger straight needle.

Knitting the Sleeves

SET UP With CA and using smaller straight needles, cast on

44 sts	48 sts	52 sts

NOTE See Two-Knit-Rib Start, page 107.

ROWS 1 AND 2 Work in Rib Stitch.

NEXT ROWS Continue in Rib Stitch, ending with a wrong-side row, until piece measures 3" (7.5 cm). Change to larger straight needles.

NEXT ROW (RIGHT-SIDE INCREASE ROW) K1 (edge stitch), M1, knit to last stitch, M1, K1 (edge stitch). You have just increased 2 stitches.

NEXT ROWS Work increase row 11 more times every	6 rows	6 rows	8 rows
You now have	68 sts	72 sts	76 sts

NEXT ROWS Work increase row every	0 rows	8 rows	6 rows
	0 more times	2 more times	4 more times
You now have	68 sts	76 sts	84 sts

NEXT ROWS Work even in Stockinette Stitch, ending with a wrong-side row, until sleeve measures from cast-on edge	18" (45.5 cm)	18" (45.5 cm)	19" (48.5 cm)

Shape Sleeve Cap

ROWS 1 AND 2 At beginning of next 2 rows, bind off	4 sts	4 sts	6 sts
You now have	60 sts	68 sts	72 sts

ROW 3 (RIGHT-SIDE DECREASE ROW) K1 (edge stitch), ssk, knit to last 3 stitches, K2tog, K1 (edge stitch). You have just decreased 2 stitches.

NEXT ROWS Work decrease row every right-side row	19 more times	22 more times	23 more times
You now have	20 sts	22 sts	24 sts

Bind off all stitches. Work second sleeve the same as the first.

Finishing

Sew sleeve and side seams. Sew sleeves into armholes, matching center-top edge of each sleeve cap to shoulder join. Fold body hems to wrong side along fold lines. Carefully remove Provisional Cast-On to expose a few live stitches at a time at lower edge, then with CA and tapestry needle, whipstitch live stitches of hem to wrong side of body (see Techniques, page 179), making sure you sew through each live stitch once to secure it and sew into the same row of the main fabric all the way across to keep stitching straight. Weave in ends.

15.25" (17.25", 18.25")

5.75" (6.5", 6.75")

2.5"

8.5" (9", 9.5")

15" (16", 16")

17.75" (20", 22")

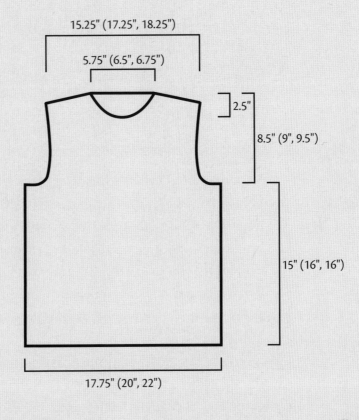

13" (14.5", 16")

3.75" (4.25", 4.5")

5.5" (6.5", 6.75")

18" (18", 19")

3"

8.5" (9", 10")

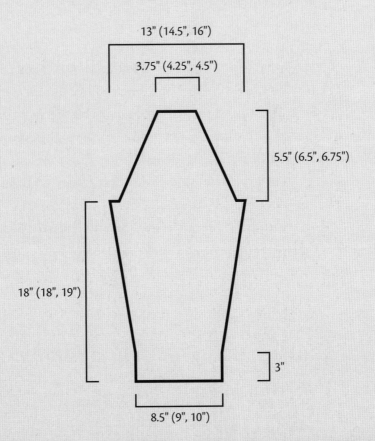

Short Rows

Short rows are used in this sweater to shape the shoulders and the neck without the "step" effect that results when you bind off at the beginning of every other row for shaping. Short rows are actually short: You'll work a specified number of stitches and stop short of finishing the row, then wrap the yarn around the next stitch, turn (wrap and turn, WT), and work back in the opposite direction. Here's how to work short rows as called for in the neck and shoulders of this sweater.

Work the number of stitches specified; this will leave some stitches unworked at the end of the row. Bring the yarn to the front of the work and slip the next stitch from the left needle to the right needle as if to purl. Bring the yarn to the back again and return the slipped stitch to the left needle. The first stitch on the left needle now has the working yarn wrapped around its base (see fig. 1).

Turn the work so the other side is facing you and continue according to the instructions. When you look at the piece from the right side, you will see that the columns of stitches on one side of the wrapped stitch have two more rows than the ones on the other side of it (see fig. 2). Continue working short rows as instructed.

When you've finished all the short rows, your knitting will be sloped, as shown in figure 3.

Now you'll have to close the gaps and hide the wraps. To hide the wraps on a right-side row in Stockinette Stitch, insert the right needle tip under the wrap from front to back and from bottom to top and then into the wrapped stitch as if to knit. Knit the stitch together with its wrap.

To hide the wraps on a wrong-side row in Stockinette Stitch, use the right needle tip to lift the back loop of the wrap from back to front and from bottom to top and place it on the left needle. Purl the stitch together with its wrap.

Once the wraps are hidden, you'll have a neatly shaped piece with live stitches for joining or picking up for neck ribbing (fig. 4).

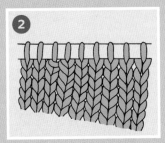
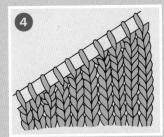
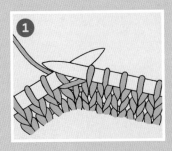
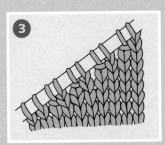

[He's Moving In]
HALF-ZIP Pullover

ARE YOU SURE HE'S THE ONE? Yes, you're moving in together, but are you really, really sure? Here's the test: Are both your names on the lease? If the answer is yes, buy the yarn for this half-zip pullover. If the answer is no, but you've convinced yourself that extenuating circumstances justify only one of your names being on the lease, then you may also proceed. But just in case, this sweater is knit in a riblike fabric that has a little give, allowing it to expand or contract to fit a few different sizes, so if Mr. Wrong walks out the door, this sweater may very well fit Mr. Right when he walks in.

The Pattern Stitch (Twisted Rib Pattern) for this sweater is easy to remember and simple to work, but be forewarned that it takes some time and really sucks up the yarn. There is no ribbing at the bottom, which is worked in the same stitch as the body of the pullover but on a smaller needle for a sleek and slightly narrower hip.

YARN
Rowan Wool Cotton, 50% merino wool, 50% cotton, 123 yd (113 m) per 50 g
Yarn band gauge: 22 to 24 stitches = 4" (10 cm) on US 5 (3.75 mm) or 6 (4 mm) needles
Color: 907 Deepest Olive, 19, 20, 21 balls, depending on size

FINISHED SIZE
40.5", 44.5", 48.5" (103, 113, 123 cm) chest. Model shown is size 44.5".

GAUGE
32 stitches and 35 rows = 4" in Pattern Stitch (Twisted Rib Pattern) on larger needles

NEEDLES
US 3 (3.25 mm) and 5 (3.75 mm) straight needles *or size you need to obtain the correct gauge*

NOTIONS
Tapestry needle, 9" (23 cm) zipper, sewing needle and matching thread for inserting zipper, straight pins, scrap yarn

ABBREVIATIONS
M1P = make 1 purl increase (see Techniques, page 181)
RT = right twist: Skip the first stitch, with the needle in *front* knit the second stitch and leave on needle; knit the first stitch and slide both stitches off needle.
LT = left twist: Skip the first stitch, with the needle *in back* knit the second stitch and leave on needle; knit the first stitch and slide both stitches off needle.

pattern stitch

Twisted Rib Pattern

IIIIIIIIIIIIII

(Multiple of 8 Stitches, Plus 2)

ROW 1 (RIGHT SIDE) *K2, P1, RT, LT, P1; repeat from * to last 2 stitches, K2.

ROW 2 (WRONG SIDE) *P2, K1, P4, K1; repeat from * to last 2 stitches, P2.

Repeat Rows 1 and 2 for pattern.

Knitting the Back

	Small	Medium	Large
SET UP With smaller needles, cast on	162 sts	178 sts	194 sts
NEXT ROWS Work in Twisted Rib Pattern until piece measures 3" (7.5 cm). Change to larger needles.			
NEXT ROWS Continue in Twisted Rib Pattern until piece measures 25" (63.5 cm) from cast-on edge for all sizes.			
Place on holders at each side for shoulders	56 sts	59 sts	63 sts
Place on another holder for back neck	50 sts	60 sts	68 sts

Knitting the Front

Work as for Back until piece measures 17" (43 cm) from cast-on edge, ending with a wrong-side row.

Dividing for Placket and Working Left Front

	Small	Medium	Large
ROW 1 Work in established pattern for Left Front	81 sts	89 sts	97 sts
Place on holder for Right Front remaining	81 sts	89 sts	97 sts
NEXT ROW (WRONG SIDE) P1, M1P, then work in established Twisted Rib Pattern to end of row. *You now have* for Left Front	82 sts	90 sts	98 sts
NEXT ROWS Work even in Twisted Rib Pattern until piece measures 22.5" (57 cm) from cast-on edge, ending with a wrong-side row.			

Shaping Left-Front Neck

	Small	Medium	Large
ROW 1 (RIGHT SIDE) Work in Pattern Stitch	66 sts	69 sts	73 sts
Place on a holder at the end of the row (neck edge) remaining	16 sts	21 sts	25 sts
NEXT ROW Turn and work one wrong-side row in established pattern on	66 sts	69 sts	73 sts
NEXT ROWS Working in established pattern, decrease 1 stitch at the end (neck edge) of the next 10 right-side rows. *You now have*	56 sts	59 sts	63 sts

NEXT ROWS Work even in established pattern, if necessary, until piece measures 25" (63.5 cm) from cast-on edge for all sizes, ending with a right-side row. Place stitches on holder.

Working Right Front

Return to larger needles for Right Front	81 sts	89 sts	97 sts

Join yarn with right side facing you.

ROW 1 (RIGHT SIDE) K1, M1, then work in established Twisted Rib Pattern to end of row. *You now have*	82 sts	90 sts	97 sts

NEXT ROWS Work even in Twisted Rib Pattern until piece measures 22.5" (57 cm) from cast-on edge, ending with a wrong-side row.

Shaping Right Front Neck

ROW 1 (RIGHT SIDE) Work in Twisted Rib Pattern	16 sts	21 sts	25 sts
and place these stitches on a holder. Continue in established pattern to end of row. *You now have*	66 sts	69 sts	73 sts

ROW 2 (WRONG SIDE) Work in established pattern to end of row.

NEXT ROWS Working in established pattern, decrease 1 stitch at the beginning (neck edge) of the next 10 right-side rows. *You now have*	56 sts	59 sts	63 sts

NEXT ROWS Work even in established pattern, if necessary, until piece measures 25" (63.5 cm) from cast-on edge for all sizes, ending with a right-side row. Place stitches on holder.

Joining the Shoulders

Using Three-Needle Bind-Off or Variation (see Techniques, pages 177–178), join stitches of Right Front and Back Shoulders. Center Back Neck stitches remain on separate holder.

Making the Collar

ROW 1 (RIGHT SIDE) Join yarn with right side facing you and knit onto larger needle from Right Front holder	16 sts	21 sts	25 sts

Pick up and knit 15 stitches for all sizes along shaped Right Front Neck edge to shoulder seam. Knit from Back Neck holder	50 sts	60 sts	68 sts
Pick up and knit 14 stitches for all sizes along shaped Left Front neck edge from shoulder seam to stitches on holder. Knit from Left Front holder	16 sts	21 sts	25 sts
You now have	111 sts	131 sts	147 sts

ROW 2 (WRONG SIDE) K2, *P1, K1; repeat from * to last 3 stitches, P1, K2.

ROW 3 (RIGHT SIDE) P2, *K1, P1; repeat from * to last 3 stitches, K1, P2.

NEXT ROWS Repeat Rows 2 and 3 until collar measures 6" (15 cm) from pickup row, ending with a wrong-side Row 2.

Right Placket Facing

ROW 1 (RIGHT SIDE) K2, P1, K1, P1, K2.

Place on a holder remaining	104 sts	124 sts	140 sts

Work remaining 7 stitches (worked in Row 1) in established rib pattern until placket measures 7" (18 cm) from where remaining stitches were placed on holder. Bind off 7 stitches.

Left Placket Facing

Return 7 stitches at opposite end of held collar stitches to larger needle and work as for Right Placket Facing. *You now have* remaining on collar holder	97 sts	117 sts	133 sts

Adding the Zipper

Fold the collar in half, bringing down the live collar stitches on the holder to meet the base of the pickup row on the wrong side of the garment. Mark the position of the fold line on either side of the center front opening with a length of yarn or safety pins. With right side facing you, bring together the edges of the front placket opening and place the closed zipper under the placket, aligning the teeth with the center front and placing the zipper stops at the top of the zipper as close as possible to collar fold line. Fold under any extra zipper tape at the top edge. Pin the zipper in place along the right and left sides of the front opening. Open the zipper.

With sewing needle and thread, sew the zipper to the sweater, stitching in the ditch between the K2 edge stitches and the adjacent purl stitch on each side of the front opening.

Fold collar and placket facings to the inside of the sweater. Pin each placket along the zipper to cover the zipper tape, but not so close that the zipper will catch the facings. Sew center front edge of each facing to the zipper with matching thread and sewing needle, then sew the other edge of each facing to the wrong side of the front using project yarn and a tapestry needle. With project yarn and tapestry needle, stitch the live stitches of the collar to the wrong side of the body along pickup row of the collar, making sure you sew through each live stitch once to secure (see Techniques, page 180).

Making the Sleeves

SET UP With smaller needles, cast on 74 stitches for all sizes.

NEXT ROWS Work in Twisted Rib Pattern until piece measures 3" (7.5 cm). Change to larger needles.

NEXT ROW (RIGHT-SIDE INCREASE ROW) K1 (edge stitch), M1, knit to last stitch, M1, K1 (edge stitch). You have just increased 2 stitches.

NEXT ROWS Incorporating new stitches into Pattern Stitch as they become established, work an increase row every 4 rows (every other right-side row) 31 more times for all sizes. *You now have* 138 stitches for all sizes.

NEXT ROWS Work even in Pattern Stitch until sleeve measures 20" (51 cm) from cast-on edge or is of desired length.

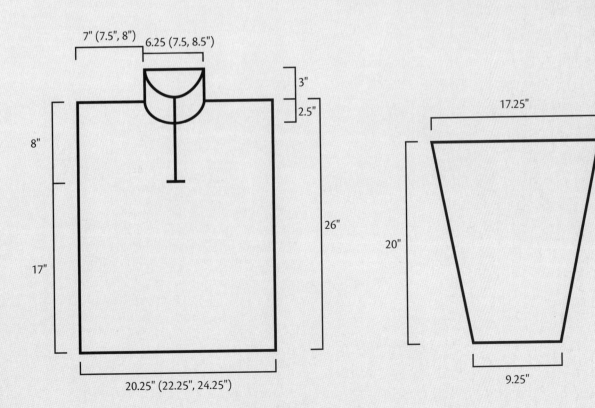

Finishing

Sew sleeves to body, matching center of sleeve bind-off row to shoulder join. Sew sleeve and side seams, weave in all ends, wash, and block.

7" (7.5", 8")

6.25 (7.5, 8.5")

3"

2.5"

8"

26"

17"

20.25" (22.25", 24.25")

17.25"

20"

9.25"

[Bells Are Ringing] DIAMOND
Classic Cardigan

WHEN THE DIAMOND (or other precious stone of your liking) is firmly planted on your finger and a date for the celebration has been chosen — and not one day before — you may begin this pièce de résistance. This sweater is loaded with challenges and is not for the faint of needles. Plan on giving him this cardigan for your first anniversary.

Featured in this sweater is Trinity Stitch, which has two parts. A "knit-purl-knit" in one stitch and a "purl three together" above it form a bobble. The bobbles are staggered in brick fashion. When setting up your sweater pieces, it's important that two pieces that are to be joined have different parts at their edges. For example, if the first row of the Left Front has a "purl three together" at the side seam, the first row of the Left Back has a "knit-purl-knit" at the side seam. This way, when you're putting together the pieces, the pattern is not interrupted at the seams. It's also important that the two edges of each piece mirror one another; the decreases should be worked on the same rows on both sides of the piece. (See Decreasing in Trinity Stitch, page 170.)

YARN
Cascade Yarns Cascade 220 Wool,
  100% Peruvian highland wool,
  220 yd (201 m) per 100 g
Yarn band gauge: 5 stitches = 1" (2.5 cm)
  on US 7 (4.5 mm) needles; 4.5 stitches =
  1" (2.5 cm) on US 8 (5 mm) needles
Color: 8400 Gray, 8, 9 skeins, depending on size

FINISHED SIZE
45", 50" (114.5, 127 cm) chest. Model shown is
  50" (127 cm).

GAUGE
20 stitches = 4" (10 cm) in Stockinette Stitch on
  larger needles; 26 stitches and 28 rows = 4"
  (10 cm) in Trinity Stitch on larger needles;
  17 stitches and 18 rows of one Diamond Cable
  repeat = 2.25" (5.5 cm) wide and 2.5" (6.5 cm)
  long on larger needles; 6 stitches of each 3/3
  Cable = 0.75" (2 cm) wide on larger needles

NEEDLES
US 6 (4 mm) and 8 (5 mm) straight needles
  and set of two size US 6 (4 mm) double-
  pointed needles *or sizes you need to obtain
  the correct gauge*

NOTIONS
Tapestry needle, cable needle, six ¾" (2 cm)
  buttons, scrap yarn, size E (3.5 mm) or
  slightly smaller crochet hook

ABBREVIATIONS
M1 = make 1 increase
  (see Techniques, page 181)
M1P = make 1 purl increase
  (see Techniques, page 181)
Pfb = purl in front and back of stitch
  (to increase)
Kfb = knit in front and back of stitch
  (to increase)
cn = cable needle

Knitting the Back

Ribbing

	Small	Large

NOTE Use 1/1 Rib Cast-On for all pieces (see Techniques, page 175). Also see Two-Knit-Rib Start, page 107.

	Small	Large
SET UP Cast on with larger needles	130 sts	144 sts

Change to smaller needles.

ROW 1 (RIGHT SIDE) K2, *P1, K1; repeat from * to end of row.

ROW 2 (WRONG SIDE) *P1, K1; repeat from * to last 2 stitches, P2.

NEXT ROWS Repeat these two rows, ending with a right-side row, until piece measures 2" (5 cm).

Setting Up for Patterns and Increasing

SET UP ROW (WRONG SIDE) Set up for Cable patterns and increase for your size as follows:

Size 45" (114.5 cm)
P1 (edge stitch), *work 4 stitches in established rib, M1; repeat from * one more time, work 2 stitches in established rib, K2, Pfb in each of next 3 stitches, **K6, Pfb, K1, Pfb, K6, Pfb in each of next 3 stitches; repeat from ** one more time, work 26 stitches in established rib, ***Pfb in each of next 3 stitches, K6, Pfb, K1, Pfb, K6; repeat from *** one more time, Pfb in each of next 3 stitches, K2, work 2 stitches in established rib, ****M1, work 4 stitches in established rib; repeat from **** one more time, P1 (edge stitch).

Size 50" (127 cm)
P1 (edge stitch), *work 4 stitches in established rib, M1; repeat from * two more times, work 1 stitch in established rib, K2, Pfb in each of next 3 stitches, **K6, Pfb, K1, Pfb, K6, Pfb in each of next 3 stitches; repeat from ** one more time, work 34 stitches in established rib, ***Pfb in each of next 3 stitches, K6, Pfb, K1, Pfb, K6; repeat from *** one more time, Pfb in each of next 3 stitches, K2, work 1 stitch in established rib, ****M1, work 4 stitches in established rib; repeat from **** two more times, P1 (edge stitch).

You now have	160 sts	176 sts

Trinity Stitch

Note: See also Decreasing in Trinity Stitch, page 170.

ROWS 1 AND 3 (RIGHT SIDE) Purl.

ROW 2 (WRONG SIDE) *P3tog; knit, purl, knit all in next stitch; repeat from * to end of row.

ROW 4 *Knit, purl, knit all in next stitch; P3tog; repeat from * to end.

Repeat Rows 1–4 for pattern.

□	k on RS; p on WS	
–	p on RS; k on WS	
•	purl 3tog	
⋀	k, p, k in 1 st	

Sl 3 sts onto cn, hold in back, K3, K3 from cn

Sl 3 sts onto cn, hold in front, K3, K3 from cn

3/3 Right Cable

(Worked over 6 Stitches)

ROWS 1 AND 5 (RIGHT SIDE) K6.

ROWS 2, 4, AND 6 (WRONG SIDE) P6.

ROW 3 Slip 3 stitches on cable needle and hold in back, K3, K3 from cable needle.

Repeat Rows 1–6 for pattern.

3/3 Left Cable

(Worked over 6 Stitches)

ROWS 1 AND 5 (RIGHT SIDE) K6.

ROWS 2, 4, AND 6 (WRONG SIDE) P6.

ROW 3 Slip 3 stitches on cable needle and hold in front, K3, K3 from cable needle.

Repeat Rows 1–6 for pattern.

Right Diamond Cable

(Worked over 17 Stitches)

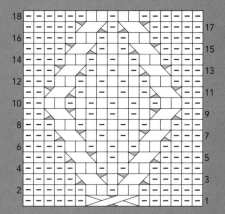

ROW 1 (RIGHT SIDE) P6, slip 3 stitches onto cable needle and hold in back, K2, slip last stitch on cable needle to left needle and purl it, K2 from cable needle, P6.

ROWS 2–18 (EVEN ROWS; WRONG SIDE) Knit the knits and purl the purls (see Techniques, page 181).

ROW 3 P5, slip 1 stitch onto cable needle and hold in back, K2, P1 from cable needle, K1, slip 2 stitches onto cable needle and hold in front, P1, K2 from cable needle, P5.

ROW 5 P4, slip 1 stitch onto cable needle and hold in back, K2, P1 from cable needle, K1, P1, K1, slip 2 stitches onto cable needle and hold in front, P1, K2 from cable needle, P4.

ROW 7 P3, slip 1 stitch onto cable needle and hold in back, K2, P1 from cable needle, *K1, P1, repeat from * one more time, K1, slip 2 stitches onto cable needle and hold in front, P1, K2 from cable needle, P3.

ROW 9 P2, slip 1 stitch onto cable needle and hold in back, K2, P1 from cable needle, *K1, P1, repeat from * two more times, K1, slip 2 stitches onto cable needle and hold in front, P1, K2 from cable needle, P2.

ROW 11 P2, slip 2 stitches onto cable needle and hold in front, P1, K2 from cable needle, *P1, K1, repeat from * two more times, P1, slip 1 stitch onto cable needle and hold in back, K2, P1 from cable needle, P2.

ROW 13 P3, slip 2 stitches onto cable needle and hold in front, P1, K2 from cable needle, *P1, K1, repeat from * one more time, P1, slip 1 stitch onto cable needle and hold in back, K2, P1 from cable needle, P3.

ROW 15 P4, slip 2 stitches onto cable needle and hold in front, P1, K2 from cable needle, P1, K1, P1, slip 1 stitch onto cable needle and hold in back, K2, P1 from cable needle, P4.

ROW 17 P5, slip 2 stitches onto cable needle and hold in front, P1, K2 from cable needle, P1, slip 1 stitch onto cable needle and hold in back, K2, P1 from cable needle, P5.

Repeat Rows 1–18 for pattern.

Begin Patterns

ROW 1 (RIGHT SIDE) Change to larger needles and K1 (edge stitch; work in Stockinette Stitch), work Row 1 of Trinity Stitch (see chart on page 151) over next   12 sts   16 sts

P2 (work in Reverse Stockinette Stitch: purl on right side, knit on wrong side), *work Row 1 of 3/3 Right Cable (see chart on page 151) over 6 stitches, work Row 1 of Right Diamond Cable (see chart on page 152) over 17 stitches; repeat from * one more time, work Row 1 of 3/3 Right Cable over 6 stitches, P1 (work in Reverse Stockinette Stitch), work Row 1 of Trinity Stitch over center   24 sts   32 sts

P1 (work in Reverse Stockinette Stitch), **work Row 1 of 3/3 Left Cable (see chart on page 151) over 6 stitches, work Row 1 of Left Diamond Cable (see chart below) over 17 stitches; repeat from ** one more time, work Row 1 of 3/3 Left Cable over 6 stitches, P2 (work in Reverse Stockinette Stitch), work Row 3 of Trinity Stitch over   12 sts   16 sts

K1 (edge stitch; work in Stockinette Stitch)

---

pattern stitch

Left Diamond Cable

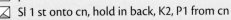
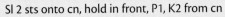

□ k on RS; p on WS
− p on RS; k on WS
Sl 1 st onto cn, hold in back, K2, P1 from cn
Sl 2 sts onto cn, hold in front, P1, K2 from cn
Sl 3 sts onto cn, hold in back, K2, sl last st on cn to left needle and purl it, K2 from cn
Sl 3 sts onto cn, hold in front, K2, sl last st on cn to left needle and purl it, K2 from cn

(Worked over 17 Stitches)

Work as for Right Diamond Cable except for the following change in Row 1:

ROW 1 (RIGHT SIDE) P6, slip 3 stitches onto cable needle and hold in front, K2, slip first stitch on cable needle to left needle and purl it, K2 from cable needle, P6.

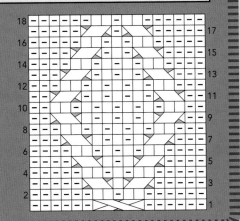

NEXT ROWS Maintaining edge stitches, work in patterns as established until piece measures 14.5" (35.5 cm) from cast-on edge for both sizes.

NOTE Be sure that you begin the first wrong-side Trinity Stitch panel with Row 4 and the center and end-of-row panels with Row 2. End having completed Row 4 of Trinity Stitch on Left Back and Row 2 of Trinity Stitch on Right Back.

Armhole Bind-Off

ROWS 1 AND 2 Continuing in established patterns, bind off 8 stitches at the beginning of the next 2 rows for both sizes.
You now have   144 sts   160 sts

At each end of the row there is 1 stitch that will become the new edge stitch, and in Trinity Stitch pattern there are   4 sts   8 sts

Armhole Decreases

NOTE As you work the armhole decreases, reestablish the edge stitches by working the first and last stitches of each row in Stockinette Stitch and continue in established patterns on center stitches.

NEXT ROWS Working decreases at both ends of the row just inside the edge stitches, repeat 4-row decreases from Decreasing in Trinity Stitch (see page 170)   1 time   2 times

There are no stitches remaining in Trinity Stitch at the ends of the row and *you now have*   136 sts   144 sts

NEXT ROWS For size 45" (114.5 cm) only, maintaining patterns, decrease 1 stitch at each end of next 4 right-side rows as follows: K1 (edge stitch), P2tog, work in pattern to last 3 stitches, P2tog, K1 (edge stitch). After last decrease row, work 1 wrong-side row even. *You now have* 128 stitches for size 45" (114.5 cm).

NEXT 2 ROWS For both sizes, work even in established patterns.

NEXT ROW (RIGHT SIDE) K1 (edge stitch), P2tog, work in pattern to last 3 stitches, P2tog, K1 (edge stitch).
You now have   126 sts   142 sts

NEXT ROWS Work even in established patterns until armholes measure approximately 9.5" (24 cm) from armhole bind-off row, ending with Row 8 of Right Diamond Cable and Left Diamond Cable.

NEXT ROW (RIGHT SIDE) To keep the piece from flaring at the shoulders, decrease each 6-stitch cable to 3 stitches as follows.

For 3/3 Right Cables, slip 3 stitches onto cable needle and hold in back, knit together the 3 stitches on cable needle and the next 3 stitches by working K2tog (one stitch each from main needle and cable needle) three times.

For 3/3 Left Cables, slip 3 stitches onto cable needle and hold in front, knit together the 3 stitches on cable needle and the next 3 stitches by working K2tog (one stitch each from main needle and cable needle) three times.

You now have	108 sts	124 sts

NEXT ROW (WRONG SIDE) Work even. Place on holders at each side for Shoulders	38 sts	42 sts

Place on another holder for Back Neck	32 sts	40 sts

Knitting the Right Front

Ribbing

SET UP Cast on with larger needles	69 sts	81 sts

Change to smaller needles.

ROW 1 (RIGHT SIDE) K1, *P1, K1; repeat from * to end.

ROW 2 (WRONG SIDE) P1, *K1, P1, repeat from * to end.

NEXT ROWS Repeat Rows 1 and 2, ending with a wrong-side row, until the piece measures 2" (5 cm) for both sizes.

NEXT ROW (RIGHT SIDE) Work 8 stitches in established K1, P1 rib and place them on a holder, then work in rib pattern to end of row. *You now have*	61 sts	73 sts

Body

SET UP ROW (WRONG SIDE) Set up for cable patterns and increase for your size as follows:

Size 45" (114.5 cm)
P1 (edge stitch), *work 4 stitches in established rib, M1; repeat from * one more time, work 1 stitch in established rib, M1, K1, Pfb in each of next 3 stitches, **K6, Pfb, K1, Pfb, K6, Pfb in each of next 3 stitches; repeat from ** one more time, K1, work 1 stitch in established rib, M1, ***work 4 stitches in established rib, M1; repeat from *** one more time, P1 (edge stitch).

Size 50" (127 cm)
P1 (edge stitch), work 4 stitches in established rib, M1, work 11 stitches in established rib, K1, Pfb in each of next 3 stitches, *K6, Pfb, K1, Pfb, K6, Pfb in each of next 3 stitches; repeat from * one more time, K1, work 11 stitches in established rib, M1, work 4 stitches in established rib, P1 (edge stitch).

You now have	80 sts	88 sts

Begin Patterns

ROW 1 (RIGHT SIDE) Change to larger needles and K1 (edge stitch; work in Stockinette Stitch), work Row 3 of Trinity Stitch over	12 sts	16 sts.

P1 (work in Reverse Stockinette Stitch).

*Work Row 1 of 3/3 Left Cable over 6 stitches, work Row 1 of Left Diamond Cable over 17 stitches; repeat from * one more time.

Work Row 1 of 3/3 Left Cable over 6 stitches, P1 (work in Reverse Stockinette Stitch).

Work Row 1 of Trinity Stitch over	12 sts	16 sts.

K1 (edge stitch; work in Stockinette Stitch).

NEXT ROWS Maintaining edge stitches, work in patterns as established until piece measures 13" (33 cm) from cast-on edge for both sizes. Place marker at neck edge.

NOTE Be sure that you begin the first wrong-side Trinity Stitch panel (at the side seam) with Row 2 and the center-front Trinity Stitch panel with Row 4. End having completed Row 2 of Trinity Stitch at side-seam edge and Row 4 of Trinity Stitch at center-front edge.

Shape Right Front Neck

NOTE See Decreasing in Trinity Stitch, page 170.

NEXT ROWS At neck edge (the beginning of right-side rows and end of wrong-side rows), work 4-row decreases for the neck edge according to Decreasing in Trinity Stitch (page 170) twice. *You now have*	72 sts	80 sts

At center-front edge there is 1 edge stitch and in Trinity Stitch pattern there are	4 sts	8 sts

NOTE The armhole shaping begins while you are still working Right Front Neck shaping. Begin armhole shaping when piece measures approximately 14.5" (37 cm) from cast-on edge, and you have just completed Row 1 of Trinity Stitch in the pattern panel located at side edge of the front (at the end of right-side rows). Check your work frequently to ensure that you do not work past the point where the armhole shaping should start.

NEXT ROWS Neck shaping continues by working 4-row decreases from Decreasing in Trinity Stitch (page 170) at neck edge	1 more time	2 more times

No stitches remain in the Trinity Stitch panel at center front, and each right-side row begins with K1 (edge stitch), P1, and a 3/3 Left Cable.

NEXT 3 ROWS Work even at neck edge, ending with a wrong-side row.

NEXT ROW (RIGHT SIDE) Decrease the 3/3 Left Cable closest to neck edge (a cable crossing row, Row 3 of cable pattern): K1, P1, slip 3 stitches onto cable needle and hold in front, K2tog, K1, K3 from cable needle, work in pattern to end — 5 stitches remain in cable.

NEXT 5 ROWS Work even in established patterns.

NEXT ROW (RIGHT SIDE) K1, P1, slip 2 stitches onto cable needle and hold in front, K2tog, K1, K2 from cable needle, work in pattern to end — 4 stitches remain in cable.

NEXT 5 ROWS Work even in established patterns.

NEXT ROW (RIGHT SIDE) K1, P1, slip 2 stitches onto cable needle and hold in front, K2tog, K2 from cable needle, work in pattern to end — 3 stitches remain in cable.

NEXT 5 ROWS Work even in established patterns.

NEXT ROW (RIGHT SIDE) K1, P1, slip 1 stitch onto cable needle and hold in front, K2tog, K1 from cable needle, work in pattern to end — 2 stitches remain in cable.

NEXT 5 ROWS Work even in established patterns.

NEXT ROW (RIGHT SIDE) K1, P1, P2tog (remaining 2 cable stitches), work in pattern to end — 1 stitch remains in cable, now converted to a purl stitch.

NEXT 3 ROWS Work even.

NEXT ROW (RIGHT SIDE) K1, P1, P2tog, work in pattern to end.

NEXT 3 ROWS Work even.

NEXT ROW (RIGHT SIDE) K1, P1, P2tog, work in pattern to end. When all neck shaping has been completed, you have removed at neck edge a total of	19 sts	23 sts

Armhole Bind-Off

NOTE The armhole shaping begins while you are still working Right Front Neck shaping. Begin armhole shaping when piece measures approximately 14.5" (37 cm) from cast-on edge and you have just completed Row 1 of Trinity Stitch in the pattern section at side edge of the front (at the end of right-side rows).

ARMHOLE BIND-OFF ROW (WRONG SIDE) Bind off 8 stitches at the beginning of the row to end with Row 2 of Trinity Stitch pattern at side edge. At side edge there is 1 edge stitch, and there remain in Trinity Stitch pattern	4 sts	8 sts

NOTE Reestablish the edge stitch at armhole by working the last stitch of each row in Stockinette Stitch and continue in established patterns on center stitches.

Armhole Decreases

NEXT ROWS Continuing established patterns and neck decreases, at armhole edge (end of right-side rows and the beginning of wrong-side rows) work 4-row decreases from Decreasing in Trinity Stitch (page 170)	1 time	2 times

ending with Row 2 of Trinity Stitch pattern at side edge. No stitches remain in Trinity Stitch panel at side edge.

NEXT ROWS For size 45" (114.5 cm), maintaining patterns, decrease 1 stitch at armhole edge on next 4 right-side rows as follows: Work in pattern to last 3 stitches, P2tog, K1 (edge stitch). After last decrease row, work 1 wrong-side row even.

For size 50" (127 cm), work even in established patterns for 8 rows.

NEXT 2 ROWS For both sizes, work even in established patterns.

NEXT ROW (RIGHT SIDE) Work in pattern to last 3 stitches, P2tog, K1 (edge stitch). When all armhole shaping has been completed, you have removed from armhole edge a total of 17 stitches for both sizes. After completing both neck and armhole shaping, *you now have*   44 sts   48 sts

NEXT ROWS Work even in established patterns until armhole measures approximately 9.5" (24 cm) from armhole bind-off row, ending with Row 8 of Left Diamond Cable pattern.

NEXT ROW (RIGHT SIDE) To keep the piece from flaring at the shoulders, decrease to 3 stitches each of the 2 remaining 6-stitch 3/3 Left Cables: Slip 3 stitches onto cable needle and hold in front, knit together the 3 stitches on cable needle and the next 3 stitches by working K2tog (one stitch each from main needle and cable needle) 3 times. *You now have*   38 sts   42 sts

NEXT ROW Work even. Place stitches on holder.

Knitting the Left Front

Ribbing

SET UP Cast on with larger needles	68 sts	80 sts

Change to smaller needles.

NEXT ROWS Work rib as for Back for 6 rows, ending with a wrong-side row.

NEXT ROW (RIGHT SIDE) Begin buttonhole: Work in rib pattern to last 4 stitches, join a 1-yard (1-meter) length of project yarn, leaving a 12" (30.5 cm) tail, and work last 4 stitches in rib with new yarn.

NEXT ROWS Working 4 stitches at center-front edge using the separate length of yarn, work even in rib pattern for 3 more rows, ending with a wrong-side row, to create a vertical slit for a buttonhole.

NEXT ROW (RIGHT SIDE) Resume working with the main ball of yarn across all stitches. Leave remaining tail from the separate length of yarn at the top of the buttonhole; the tails will be used later to reinforce the buttonholes.

NEXT ROWS Continue in rib pattern until piece measures 2" (5 cm) for both sizes, ending with a wrong-side row.

NEXT ROW (RIGHT SIDE) Work in pattern to last 8 stitches. Place last 8 stitches on holder. *You now have*	60 sts	72 sts

Body

SET UP ROW (WRONG SIDE) Set up for cable and increase for your size as follows:

Size 45" (114.5 cm
P1 (edge stitch), *M1, work 4 stitches in established rib; repeat from * one more time, M1, work 1 stitch in established rib, M1, Pfb in each of the next 3 stitches, **K6, Pfb, K1, Pfb, K6, Pfb in each of the next 3 stitches; repeat from ** one more time, K1, work 1 stitch in established rib, M1, ***work 4 stitches in established rib, M1; repeat from *** one more time, P1 (edge stitch).

Size 50" (127 cm)
P1 (edge stitch), work 4 stitches in established rib, M1, work 10 stitches in established rib, M1, K1, Pfb in each of next 3 stitches, *K6, Pfb, K1, Pfb, K6, Pfb in each of next 3 stitches; repeat from * one more time, K1, work 11 stitches in established rib, M1, work 4 stitches in established rib, P1 (edge stitch).

You now have	80 sts	88 sts

Begin Patterns

ROW 1 (RIGHT SIDE) Change to larger needles and K1 (edge stitch; work in Stockinette Stitch), work Row 3 of Trinity Stitch over

12 sts	16 sts

P1 (work in Reverse Stockinette), *work Row 1 of 3/3 Right Cable over 6 stitches, work Row 1 of Right Diamond Cable over 17 stitches; repeat from * one more time, work Row 1 of 3/3 Right Cable over 6 sts, P1 (work in Reverse Stockinette Stitch), work Row 1 of Trinity Stitch over

12 sts	16 sts

K1 (edge stitch; work in Stockinette Stitch).

NEXT ROWS Maintaining edge stitches, work in patterns as established until piece measures 13" (33 cm) from cast-on edge for both sizes. Place marker at neck edge.

NOTE Be sure that you begin the first wrong-side Trinity Stitch panel (at the center front) with Row 2 and the Trinity Stitch panel at the side seam with Row 4, and end having just completed Row 2 of Trinity Stitch in the pattern panel located at the center-front edge of the sweater (at the end of right-side rows).

Shape Left-Front Neck

NOTE See Decreasing in Trinity Stitch (page 170).

NEXT ROWS At neck edge (the end of right-side rows and the beginning of wrong-side rows), work 4-row decreases according to Decreasing in Trinity Stitch two times. *You now have*

72 sts	80 sts

At center-front edge there is 1 edge stitch and in Trinity Stitch pattern there are

4 sts	8 sts

NOTE The armhole shaping begins while you are still working the Left Front Neck shaping. Begin the armhole shaping when the piece measures approximately 14.5" (37 cm) from cast-on edge and you have just completed Row 2 of Trinity Stitch in the pattern section located at side edge of front (at the beginning of right-side rows). Check your work frequently to ensure that you do not work past the point where armhole shaping should start.

NEXT ROWS Neck shaping continues by working Rows 1–4 from Decreasing in Trinity Stitch at neck edge

1 more time	2 more times

No stitches remain in the Trinity Stitch panel at center front and each right-side row ends with a 3/3 Right Cable followed by P1, K1 (edge stitch).

NEXT 3 ROWS Work even at neck edge, ending with a wrong-side row.

NEXT ROW (RIGHT SIDE) Decrease the 3/3 Right Cable closest to neck edge (a cable crossing row, Row 3 of cable pattern): Work in pattern to last 6-stitch cable, slip 3 stitches onto cable needle and hold in back, K3, (K2tog, K1) from cable needle, P1, K1 — 5 stitches remain in cable.

NEXT 5 ROWS Work even in established patterns.

NEXT ROW Work in pattern to last cable, slip 3 stitches onto cable needle and hold in back, K2, (K2tog, K1) from cable needle, P1, K1 — 4 stitches remain in cable.

NEXT 5 ROWS Work even in established patterns.

NEXT ROW Work in pattern to last cable, slip 2 stitches onto cable needle and hold in back, K2, K2tog from cable needle, P1, K1 — 3 stitches remain in cable.

NEXT 5 ROWS Work even in established patterns.

NEXT ROW Work in pattern to last cable, slip 2 stitches onto cable needle and hold in back, K1, K2tog from cable needle, P1, K1 — 2 stitches remain in cable.

NEXT 5 ROWS Work even in established patterns.

NEXT ROW Work in pattern to cable, P2tog (remaining 2 cable stitches), P1, K1 — 1 stitch remains in cable, now converted to a purl stitch.

NEXT 3 ROWS Work even.

NEXT ROW (RIGHT SIDE) Work in pattern to last 4 stitches, P2tog, P1, K1.

NEXT 3 ROWS Work even.

NEXT ROW (RIGHT SIDE) Work in pattern to last 4 stitches, P2tog, P1, K1.

When all neck shaping has been completed, you have removed at neck edge a total of	19 sts	23 sts

Armhole Bind-Off

NOTE The armhole shaping begins while you are still working Left Front Neck shaping. Begin armhole shaping when piece measures approximately 14.5" (37 cm) from cast-on edge and you have just completed Row 2 of Trinity Stitch in the pattern section located at side edge of the front (at the beginning of right-side rows).

ARMHOLE BIND-OFF ROW (RIGHT SIDE) Bind off 8 stitches at the beginning of the next right-side row. At side edge there will remain in Trinity Stitch pattern   4 sts   8 sts

NEXT ROW (WRONG SIDE) Work in established patterns and end with Row 4 of Trinity Stitch pattern at side edge.

NOTE Reestablish the edge stitches by working the first and last stitches of each row in Stockinette Stitch and continue in established patterns on center stitches.

Armhole Decreases

NEXT ROWS Continuing established patterns and neck decreases, at armhole edge (beginning of right-side rows and end of wrong-side rows), work 4-row decreases from Decreasing in Trinity Stitch (page 170)   1 time   2 times

ending with Row 4 of Trinity Stitch pattern at side edge. No stitches remain in Trinity Stitch panel at side edge.

NEXT ROWS For size 45" (114.5 cm), maintaining patterns, decrease 1 stitch at armhole edge on next 4 right-side rows as follows: K1 (edge stitch), P2tog, work in pattern to end. After last decrease row, work 1 wrong-side row even.

For size 50" (127 cm), work even in established patterns for 8 rows.

NEXT 2 ROWS For both sizes, work even in established patterns.

NEXT ROW (RIGHT SIDE) K1 (edge stitch), P2tog, work to end in pattern.

When all armhole shaping has been completed, you have removed from armhole edge a total of 17 stitches for both sizes. After completing both neck and armhole shaping, *you now have*   44 sts   48 sts

NEXT ROWS Work even in established patterns until armhole measures approximately 9.5" (24 cm) from armhole bind-off row, ending with Row 8 of Left Diamond Cable pattern.

NEXT ROW (RIGHT SIDE) To keep the piece from flaring at the shoulders, decrease to 3 stitches each of the two remaining 6-stitch 3/3 Right Cables: Slip 3 stitches onto cable needle and hold in back, knit together the 3 stitches on cable needle and the next 3 stitches by working K2tog (one stitch each from main needle and cable needle) three times. *You now have*   38 sts   42 sts

NEXT ROW (WRONG SIDE) Work even.

Place stitches on holder.

Joining the Shoulders

Using Three-Needle Bind-Off Variation (see Technique, page 178) and larger needle, join stitches of Right Front and Back Shoulders. Join stitches of Left Front and Back Shoulders in the same manner. Center Back Neck stitches remain on separate holder.

Making the Left Sleeve

Ribbing

SET UP Cast on with larger needles 56 stitches for both sizes. Change to smaller needles.

NEXT ROWS Work in rib as for Back until piece measures 2.25" (5.5 cm), ending with a right-side row.

SET UP ROW (WRONG SIDE) Set up for cable patterns and increase as follows: P1 (edge stitch), K1, P1, K6, Pfb, K1, Pfb, K6, Pfb in each of next 3 stitches, K6, Pfb, M1, Pfb, K6, Pfb in each of next 3 stitches, K6, Pfb, K1, Pfb, K6, P1, K1, P1 (edge stitch). *You now have 69 stitches for both sizes.*

Begin Patterns

ROW 1 (RIGHT SIDE) Change to larger needles and K1 (edge stitch; work in Stockinette Stitch), P1, K1, work Row 1 of Right Diamond Cable over 17 stitches, work Row 1 of 3/3 Right Cable over 6 stitches, work Row 1 of Right Diamond Cable over 17 stitches, work Row 1 of 3/3 Left Cable over 6 stitches, work Row 1 of Right Diamond Cable over 17 stitches, K1, P1, K1 (edge stitch; work in Stockinette Stitch).

ROWS 2–4 Working stitches at each end of row as they appear (knit the knits and purl the purls), work 3 rows even in pattern, ending with a wrong-side row.

ROW 5 (RIGHT SIDE) K1, P1, Kfb, work in pattern to last 3 stitches, increase by knitting into front and back of next stitch, P1, K1 — 2 stitches increased.

ROWS 6–8 Work 3 rows even in pattern.

ROWS 9–24 Repeat Rows 5–8 four more times.

ROW 25 Work even in established patterns.

You now have 79 stitches, with a 6-stitch stockinette panel at each end of rows where you have been increasing. From here on, work the 6-stitch panel at beginning of right-side rows in 3/3 Right Cable pattern and work the 6-stitch panel at end of right-side rows in 3/3 Left Cable pattern, crossing the new cables on the same row as the cables already established.

ROWS 26–28 Work 3 rows even in pattern.

ROW 29 (RIGHT SIDE) K1, P1, M1P, work in pattern to last 2 stitches, M1P, P1, K1 — 2 stitches increased.

ROWS 30–32 Work 3 rows even in pattern.

ROW 33 K1, P2, Kfb, work in pattern to last 3 stitches, Kfb, P2, K1 — 2 stitches increased.

ROWS 34–36 Work 3 rows even in pattern.

ROWS 37–56 Repeat Rows 33–36 five more times.

You now have 93 stitches, with a 6-stitch stockinette panel at each end of row where you have been increasing. From here on, work new 6-stitch panels as 3/3 Right Cable at beginning of row and 3/3 Left Cable at end of row, crossing the new cables on the same row as the cables already established.

ROW 57 (RIGHT SIDE) K1, M1P, work in pattern to last stitch, M1P, K1 — 2 stitches increased.

ROWS 58–60 Work 3 rows even in pattern.

ROWS 61–80 Repeat Rows 57–60 five more times.

You now have 105 stitches, with 6 purl stitches between each edge stitch and outermost cable.

ROW 81 (RIGHT SIDE) K1, work Row 1 of Trinity Stitch over next 4 stitches, M1P, P2, work in pattern to last 7 stitches, P2, M1P, work Row 3 of Trinity Stitch over next 4 stitches, K1 — 2 stitches increased.

ROWS 82–84 Work 3 rows even in pattern.

NOTE Be sure that on Row 82 (wrong side) you work Row 4 of the Trinity Stitch panel on the left side of the sleeve and Row 2 of the Trinity Stitch panel on the right side of the sleeve.

ROWS 83–96 Continue to increase 1 stitch using M1P at the end of first Trinity Stitch panel and beginning of second Trinity Stitch panel every 4th row three more times, working new stitches into Trinity Stitch pattern as soon as there are a multiple of 4 stitches and maintaining 2 stitches in Reverse Stockinette Stitch between the outermost cables and the Trinity Stitch panels.

You now have 113 stitches, with 8 stitches in Trinity Stitch panels just inside edge stitches at each end of row.

ROWS 87–102 Continue to increase 1 stitch using M1P at the end of first Trinity Stitch panel and beginning of second Trinity Stitch panel every right-side row eight more times, working new stitches into Trinity Stitch pattern and maintaining 2 stitches in Reverse Stockinette Stitch between the outermost cables and the Trinity Stitch panels.

You now have 129 stitches, with 16 stitches in Trinity Stitch panels just inside edge stitches at each end of row.

NEXT ROWS Work even in patterns until piece measures 18" (45.5 cm) from cast-on edge, ending with Row 2 of Trinity Stitch pattern on right side of sleeve.

Armhole Bind-Off

NEXT 2 ROWS Continuing in established patterns, bind off 8 stitches at the beginning of the next 2 rows for both sizes, ending with Row 4 of Trinity Stitch pattern on right side of sleeve.

You now have 113 stitches, with 8 stitches in Trinity Stitch panels at each end of row.

Armhole Decreases

NOTE Reestablish the edge stitches by working the first and last stitches of each row in Stockinette Stitch, and continue in established patterns on center stitches.

NEXT ROW Working decreases at both ends of the row just inside the edge stitches, repeat 4-row decreases from Decreasing in Trinity Stitch (see page 170) four times, ending with Row 4 of Trinity Stitch pattern on right side of sleeve and Row 2 of Trinity Stitch pattern on left side of sleeve.

You now have 97 stitches, at each side there is 1 edge stitch, and there are no stitches remaining in Trinity Stitch at each end of row.

NEXT ROWS Work even in established patterns until sleeve measures approximately 2" (5 cm) from armhole bind-off row, ending with Row 8 of the Diamond Cable pattern.

To keep the piece from flaring at the top edge, decrease to 3 stitches each 6-stitch cable as follows.

For 3/3 Right Cables, slip 3 stitches onto cable needle and hold in back, knit together the 3 stitches on cable needle and the next 3 stitches by working K2tog (one stitch each from main needle and cable needle) three times.

For 3/3 Left Cables, slip 3 stitches onto cable needle and hold in front, knit together the 3 stitches on cable needle and the next 3 stitches by working K2tog (one stitch each from main needle and cable needle) three times.

You now have 79 stitches. Bind off all stitches in pattern.

Making the Right Sleeve

Work as for Left Sleeve until the increase row above the ribbing is complete. *You now have* 69 stitches for both sizes.

Establish Patterns

ROW 1 (RIGHT SIDE) Change to larger needles and K1 (edge stitch; work in Stockinette Stitch), P1, K1, work Row 1 of Left Diamond Cable over 17 stitches, work Row 1 of 3/3 Right Cable over 6 stitches, work Row 1 of Left Diamond Cable over 17 stitches, work Row 1 of 3/3 Left Cable over 6 stitches, work Row 1 of Left Diamond Cable over 17 stitches, K1, P1, K1 (edge stitch; work in Stockinette Stitch).

NEXT ROWS Work as for Left Sleeve in established patterns.

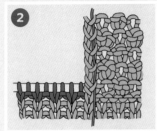

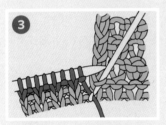

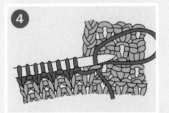

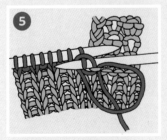

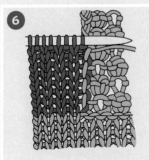

Making the Front Band and Neck Band

SET UP Mark the positions for six buttons along edge of Right Front, with the lowest corresponding to the buttonhole in the ribbing on Left Front, the highest positioned 0.5" (1.3 cm) below beginning of the neck shaping, and the remaining four buttons spaced evenly in between.

Making the Left-Front Band

ROW 1 Place 8 held stitches from lower edge of Left Front on double-pointed needle and join yarn at body edge with right side facing you, ready to work a right-side row. Work 8 stitches in established rib pattern (fig. 1). Turn.

ROW 2 (WRONG SIDE) Work in established rib. Turn.

NOTE The vertical line of edge stitches along the center-front edge of the body consists of a series of alternating loose and tight stitches. The tight stitches are threaded on a contrasting scrap yarn to identify them in figure 2.

Insert crochet hook through the first tight loop above the ribbing and pull through a loop of the working yarn (figs. 3 and 4).

NOTE If you pull on one end of the loop, it grows larger, and if you pull on the other end, it is securely attached to the work. The attached end is shown above the needle in figure 4.

ROW 3 (RIGHT SIDE) Pull out enough slack in the loop so you can work freely, and using the attached end, work in pattern over the 8 rib stitches of the front band, turn.

ROW 4 (WRONG SIDE) Work in pattern over the same 8 stitches to end back at the inner edge of the band, between the band and the body of the sweater (fig. 5).

Pull on the working yarn until the excess loop disappears completely, adjusting the tension to match the stitches.

NEXT ROWS Use the crochet hook to draw up a new loop in the next front edge stitch above and repeat the process, working 2 rows on the rib band with each loop. Working the band in this manner eliminates any guesswork — you are working row for row and attaching the band to the garment on every other row (fig. 6).

Continue in this manner, until front band is almost even with the next marked button position on Right Front.

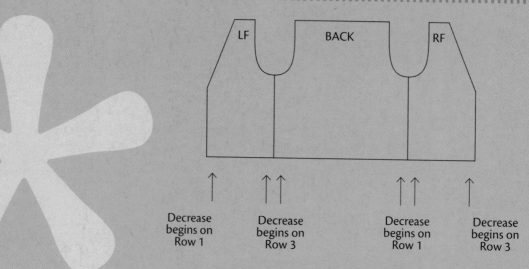

LF   BACK   RF

Decrease begins on Row 1

Decrease begins on Row 3

Decrease begins on Row 1

Decrease begins on Row 3

Decreasing in Trinity Stitch

In order to maintain the staggered bobbles in Trinity Stitch, decreases are worked over four rows, beginning on a right-side row. The decreases are always worked in the stitches that sit above a bobble from the previous row.

Some of the instructions in this pattern call for you to begin the Trinity Stitch with pattern Row 1, some instructions call for you to begin on pattern Row 3. Regardless of where you start, the decreases are always worked on the same pattern rows as follows: *Decreases worked at the beginning of a Trinity Stitch panel start on pattern Row 1. Decreases worked at the end of a Trinity Stitch panel start on pattern Row 3.*

To decrease at the beginning of a Trinity Stitch panel, work as follows.

PATTERN ROW 1 P2tog, purl to end of Trinity Stitch panel.

PATTERN ROW 2 Work in established pattern to last 3 stitches of Trinity Stitch panel, P3tog.

PATTERN ROW 3 P2tog, purl to end of Trinity Stitch panel.

PATTERN ROW 4 Reestablish Trinity Stitch by working this row even in pattern.

To decrease at the end of a Trinity Stitch panel, work as follows:

PATTERN ROW 3 Purl to last 2 stitches of Trinity Stitch panel, P2tog.

PATTERN ROW 4 P3tog, work to end of Trinity Stitch panel in established pattern.

PATTERN ROW 1 Purl to last 2 stitches of Trinity Stitch panel, P2tog.

PATTERN ROW 2 Reestablish Trinity Stitch by working this row even in pattern.

The net result for both of these scenarios is that you have decreased 4 stitches (1 bobble) in 4 rows. The diagram above shows mirror-image decreases. Decreasing at the beginning of the Trinity Stitch panel on the right begins on pattern Row 1. Decreasing at the end of the Trinity Stitch panel on the left begins on pattern Row 3.

Making the Buttonholes

SET UP On next right-side row, work in rib pattern using loop to last 4 stitches, join a 1-yard (1 meter) length of project yarn and, leaving a 12" (30.5 cm) tail, work last 4 stitches in rib with new yarn. Turn, work 4 stitches with separate yarn, then work 4 stitches with loop.

NEXT 2 ROWS Work in the same manner, ending with a wrong-side row, to create a 4-row vertical slit for buttonhole.

NEXT ROW Resume working with the loop across all stitches, leaving a tail of separate yarn at the top of the buttonhole to be used later for reinforcing buttonhole.

NEXT ROWS Continue working the front band in this manner until all six buttonholes have been completed. Work even until you reach the marker for beginning of V-neck shaping on Left Front. Work short rows as follows to turn the corner and prevent the band from curling at the angle of the V-neck (see Short Rows, pages 138–139).

ROWS 1 AND 2 Work 6 stitches in rib, wrap next stitch and turn work (WT), work 6 stitches in rib.

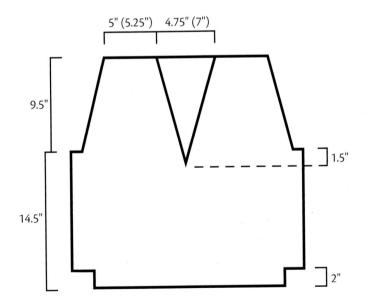

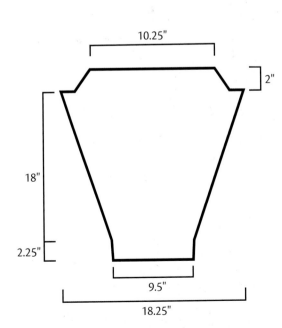

ROWS 3 AND 4 Work 2 rows even across all 8 Front Band stitches.

ROWS 5 AND 6 Repeat Rows 1 and 2.

NEXT ROWS Continue working the front band on all 8 stitches until band reaches the Left Shoulder. Work even on 8 band stitches without joining to body until band, when slightly stretched, reaches to center of held-back Neck stitches. Place 8 stitches of front band on holder.

Making the Right-Front Band

SET UP Place 8 held stitches from lower edge of Right Front on double-pointed needle and, with wrong-side facing you, join yarn to body edge of Right Front and work 1 wrong-side row in established rib across 8 stitches. Turn work and rib 8 stitches, ending at body edge. Drawing up loops from the Right Front body edge as for Left Front Band, work each pair of Front Band rows as first a wrong-side row, then a right-side row, to end back at the inner edge of the band between the band and the body of the sweater. Continue in this manner until you reach the marker for beginning of V-neck shaping on Right Front. Work short rows as for Left Front band.

NEXT ROWS Continue working the front band on all 8 stitches until band reaches Right Shoulder. Work even in rib on 8 band stitches without joining to body until band, when slightly stretched, reaches to center of held-back Neck stitches. Return stitches of left band to double-pointed needle and use Three-Needle Bind-Off (see Techniques, page 177) or Kitchener Stitch (see Techniques, page 179) to join live stitches from each half of band.

Finishing

Whipstitch live stitches of Center Back Neck to edge of Neck Band, making sure you sew through each live stitch once to secure it. Sew sleeve and side seams. Sew sleeves into armholes, matching center top edge of each sleeve cap to shoulder join. Weave in ends. Sew buttons on Right Front band to correspond with buttonholes. Reinforce buttonholes using the Buttonhole Stitch (see Techniques, page 179).

Techniques

Casting On

There are many ways to cast on. You should choose your method based on the look you want and the method you're most comfortable using.

Cable Cast-On

This is an all-purpose cast-on using two needles.

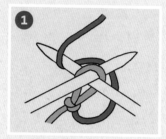

1. Make a slip knot and place it on the needle. With a second needle, knit into the slip knot to form a new stitch (fig. 1).

2. Pull this stitch long and place it on the first needle with the slip knot (fig. 2).

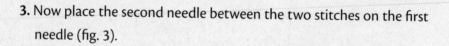

3. Now place the second needle between the two stitches on the first needle (fig. 3).

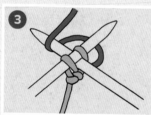

4. Knit a new stitch between the two stitches, pull it long, and place in on the first needle (fig. 4).

5. Continue in this manner, knitting between the last two stitches on the first needle, until you've cast on the desired number of stitches.

Long-Tail Cast-On

This is an all-purpose cast-on using one needle.

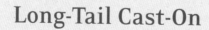

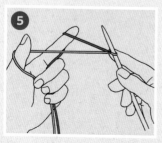

1. Leaving a tail long enough to cast on the desired number of stitches (a generous guess is 1 inch per stitch), make a slip knot and place it on the needle. Wrap one of the threads around your thumb and the other around your index finger. Hold the tails with your other three fingers (fig. 5).

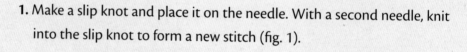

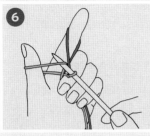

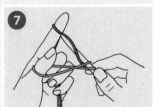

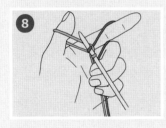

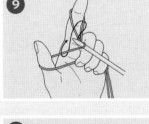

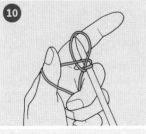

2. Insert needle into the loop around your thumb from front to back and over the yarn around your index finger (figs. 6 and 7).

3. Figure 6 shows the needle going into the loop on the thumb and figure 7 shows the needle tip going over the yarn on the index finger.

4. With the needle, bring the yarn from in front of your index finger down through the loop around your thumb (fig. 8).

5. Drop the loop off your thumb, tighten the stitch, and form a new loop around your thumb.

1/1 Rib Cast-On

This is a version of the Long-Tail Cast-On that results in a K1, P1 edge.

1. For the first stitch (a knit stitch), work as for the Long-Tail Cast-On, above.

2. For the second stitch (a purl stitch), insert the needle through the yarn that runs between the index and middle fingers from back to front, then down through the yarn that comes off the back of the thumb from back to front (fig. 9).

3. Finally, bring the yarn up through the loop on the index finger and tighten stitch (fig. 10).

Techniques [continued]

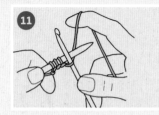

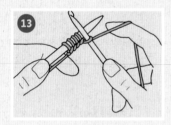

Provisional Cast-On

There are several ways to do a Provisional Cast-On. This is a favorite: Cast on using scrap yarn, then knit into these stitches with the project yarn. When you're ready to use the stitches, carefully remove the scrap yarn from the base of the main fabric and place the exposed live stitches on a needle, ready to work in the opposite direction. Follow the directions below for a Provisional Cast-On that quickly unzips from the bottom of your knitting.

1. Make a slip knot and place it on a crochet hook. Hold your knitting needle on top of a long strand of yarn (fig. 11).

2. *With the crochet hook, draw the yarn over the needle and through the loop on the hook. To cast on another stitch, bring yarn behind knitting needle into position as for step 1 and repeat from * (figs. 12 and 13). *Note:* If you find it awkward to cast on the first couple of stitches, work a few crochet chain stitches before casting onto the needle so you have something to hold on to.

3. When the last stitch has been cast on, work two or three extra crochet chain stitches without taking the yarn around the knitting needle, then cut the yarn, leaving a 10" (25.5 cm) tail; draw the tail through the last loop on the hook; and pull the tail to close the loop loosely — just enough so the tail can't escape. To remove the scrap yarn when you've finished the knitting, pull the tail out of the last loop and gently tug on it to "unzip" the chain, and carefully place the live stitches on a needle, holder, or separate length of scrap yarn as they are released.

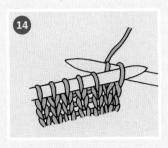

Binding Off

Regular Bind-Off

This bind-off is the same as the one you'll find in many knitting books, with the exception of the start and the finish. The instructions here should prevent the "rabbit ears" that often appear at the beginning and end of the bind-off row.

1. With the stitches to be bound off on the left needle, slip the first stitch to the empty right needle as if to knit. Knit the next stitch. Lift the slipped stitch over the knitted stitch and off the right needle (fig. 14).

2. Knit the next stitch and lift the first stitch on the right needle over this newly knitted stitch. Continue in this manner until you have one stitch left on each of the right and left needles.

3. Slip the last stitch on the left needle to the right needle as if to knit. Lift the first stitch on the right needle over the slipped stitch and off the needle, pulling down slightly on the working yarn. Cut the yarn, leaving a tail for seaming, and draw the tail through the remaining stitch.

Three-Needle Bind-Off

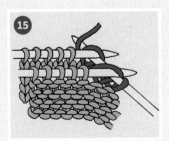

1. Place the two sets of live stitches to be bound off on separate needles. Hold the needles parallel in your left hand with right sides of the knitted fabric touching.

2. Insert the tip of a third needle into the first stitch on both needles and knit these two stitches together (fig. 15).

Techniques [continued]

3. Repeat step 2. *You now have* two stitches on the right needle. With one of the needles in your left hand, lift the first stitch on the right needle over the second and off the needle as for a regular bind off (see figure 14 under Bind Off). Repeat until all stitches are bound off.

Three-Needle Bind-Off Variation

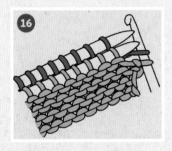

This bind off is similar to the Three-Needle Bind-Off, but it uses a crochet hook instead of a third needle. Because one set of stitches is pulled through the other, there is no extra row created between two live rows, making it especially well suited for binding off in rib or another textured pattern.

1. With right sides touching, place together the needles with stitches to be bound off as for step 1 of the Three-Needle Bind-Off.

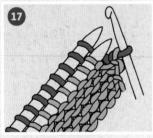

2. Insert the crochet hook into the first stitch on the front needle as if to knit and slide the stitch off the needle and onto the hook. Insert the hook into the first stitch on the back needle as if to knit and slide that stitch onto the hook (fig. 16).

3. Pull the loop on the hook from the back needle through the loop on the hook from the front needle (fig. 17).

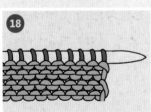

4. Repeat steps 2 and 3 until all stitches have been removed from the knitting needles. As the crochet hook fills up, transfer the stitches from the end of the crochet hook to a needle (fig. 18).

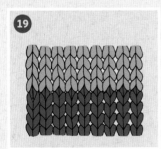

5. Now use a regular bind-off (page 177) on the one set of remaining stitches.

6. This bind-off method will result in a seam with no extra row between the last two rows of knitting (fig. 19).

Finishing

Buttonhole Stitch

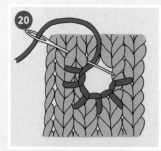

This stitch reinforces the buttonhole. Insert a threaded needle into and out of a stitch that edges the buttonhole, place the working yarn under the needle tip, then pull the needle completely through the stitch and tighten. Repeat around the circumference of the buttonhole, remembering always to place the working yarn under the needle (fig. 20).

Invisible Seam 1

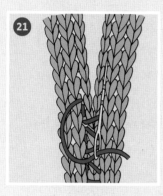

This method is characterized by a one-stitch seam allowance.

1. With a threaded tapestry needle and working from the bottom of the garment to the top, go under two bars between the first and second stitches on one edge, then under the two corresponding bars between the first and second stitches on the other edge.

2. Continue in this manner, pulling the yarn upward in the direction of the seaming to draw the two pieces together with an invisible join. Try to match the tension of the knitted fabric and don't pull the seaming yarn so tight that the seam puckers (fig. 21).

Invisible Seam 2

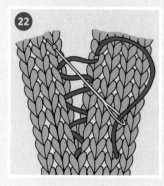

This method is characterized by a one-half-stitch seam allowance. Work as for Invisible Seam 1, but pick up only one bar from the center of each stitch by inserting your tapestry needle just below the base of the V (fig. 22).

Kitchener Stitch

This grafting technique joins two sets of live stitches invisibly. It is most often used for sock toes, but can be used to join shoulder seams or two halves of a scarf.

Techniques [continued]

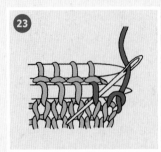

1. Place on separate needles the two sets of live stitches to be bound off. Hold the needles parallel in your left hand with right sides of the knitted fabric touching.

2. Insert a threaded tapestry needle into the first stitch on the front needle as if to purl and leave the stitch on the needle. Then insert the tapestry needle through the first stitch on the back needle as if to knit and leave the stitch on the needle.

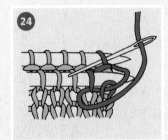

3. Insert the tapestry needle into the first stitch on the front needle as if to knit and slip the stitch off the needle. Then insert the tapestry needle into the next stitch on the front needle as if to purl and leave the stitch on the needle (fig. 23).

4. Insert the tapestry needle into the first stitch on the back needle as if to purl and slip the stitch off the needle (fig. 24).

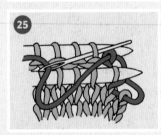

5. Insert the tapestry needle into the next stitch on the back needle as if to knit and leave the stitch on the needle (fig. 25).

6. Repeat steps 2, 3, and 4 until all stitches have been joined.

Grafting Live Stitches to the Inside of a Garment

1. Turn your hem with the live stitches to the inside and determine which row of knitted stitches it will be grafted to.

2. Insert a threaded tapestry needle into the first stitch of that knitted row, then through the first live stitch on the hem. Insert the needle into the next stitch of the same knitted row and through the next live stitch (fig. 26). Continue in this manner, working stitch for stitch, until hem is complete.

3. If you find it difficult to keep the stitches in the right place on the knitted fabric, mark the row by passing a smooth string through the row below the one to which you're stitching.

Increasing

Make 1 Increase (M1)

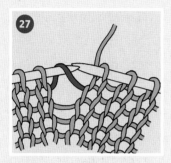

1. Work in pattern to where you'll need to begin increasing. Insert the tip of the right needle from back to front underneath the strand of yarn between the two needles and place the lifted strand on the left needle (fig. 27).
2. Knit the lifted strand through its back loop, twisting it to avoid leaving a hole (fig. 28).

Make 1 Purl Increase (M1P)

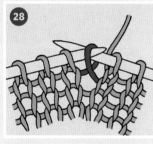

1. Work in pattern to where you'll need to begin increasing. Insert the tip of the left needle from front to back underneath the strand of yarn between the two needles (fig. 29).
2. Purl the lifted strand through its back loop, twisting it to avoid leaving a hole (fig. 30).

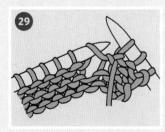

Knit the Knits and Purl the Purls

This shorthand description is often used for the wrong-side rows of textured patterns. It means simply that you work the stitches as they appear on your needles. For example, if a stitch was knitted on the right-side row, it appears as a purl on the wrong side and should be purled on the wrong-side row.

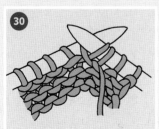

Abbreviations

cm	centimeter(s)
cn	cable needle
dpn	double-pointed needle(s)
g	gram(s)
K	knit
Kfb	knit in front and back of stitch
K2tog	knit two stitches together
m	meter(s)
M1	make one knit increase (see Techniques, page 181)
M1P	make one purl increase (see Techniques, page 181)
P	purl
Pfb	purl in front and back of stitch
pm	place marker
P2tog	purl two stitches together
rem	remain, remaining
sl	slip
ssk	slip one stitch, slip one stitch, knit the two stitches together through their back loops
st(s)	stitch, stitches
tog	together
wt	wrap and turn
wyib	with yarn in back
wyif	with yarn in front

Resources

Brown Sheep Company
100662 County Road 16
Mitchell, NE 69537
(800) 826-9136
www.brownsheep.com
Yarn used: Nature Spun Sport

Cascade Yarns, Inc.
P.O. Box 58168
Tukwila, WA 98138
(800) 548-1048
www.cascadeyarns.com
Yarn used: Cascade 220

Classic Elite Yarns
122 Western Avenue
Lowell, MA 01851
(978) 458-2837
www.classiceliteyarns.com
Yarns used: Renaissance, Wings

Dale of Norway, Inc.
4750 Shelburne Road, Suite 2
Shelburne, VT 05482
(802) 383-0132
www.dale.no
Yarn used: Dalegarn Baby Ull

Karabella Yarns
1201 Broadway
New York, NY 10001
(800) 550-0898
www.karabellayarns.com
Yarn used: Aurora 8

Knitting Fever, Inc.
P.O. Box 336
315 Bayview Avenue
Amityville, NY 11701
(516) 546-3600
www.knittingfever.com
Yarn used: Noro Big Kureyon

Louet Sales
808 Commerce Park Drive
Ogdensburg, NY 13669
(613) 925-4502
or RR 4
Prescott, ON K0E 1T0
Canada
www.louet.com
Yarn used: Gems Topaz

Norwegian Spirit, Inc.
N27 W23713 Paul Road, Unit G
Pewaukee, WI 53072
(262) 347-0809
www.spirit-norway.com
Yarn used: Lanett Superwash

Patons Yarns
320 Livingstone Avenue South
Listowel, ON N4W 3H3
Canada
(888) 368-8401
www.patonsyarns.com
Yarn used: Classic Merino Wool

Reynolds Yarn, A Division of JCA, Inc.
35 Scales Lane
Townsend, MA 01469
(978) 597-8794
Yarns used: Lite-Lopi, Saucy

Tahki • Stacy Charles, Inc.
70-30 80th Street, Building 36
Ridgewood, NY 11385
(800) 338-YARN
www.tahkistacycharles.com
Yarn used: Tahki Cotton Classic

Unicorn Books and Crafts, Inc.
1338 Ross Street
Petaluma, CA 94954
(707) 762-3362
www.unicornbooks.com
Yarn used: Lana Grossa
    Pashmina

Westminster Fibers, Inc.
4 Townsend West, Suite 8
Nashua, NH 03063
(603) 886-5041
www.westminsterfibers.com
Yarns used: Jaeger Extra Fine Merino
    DK, Jaeger Matchmaker, Rowan
    4-Ply Soft, Rowan Wool Cotton

Wooly West
P.O. Box 58306
Salt Lake City, UT 84158
(888) 487-9665
www.woolywest.com
Yarn used: Wendy Guernsey

Acknowledgments

Knitting garments and writing a manuscript are only part of what happened here — it takes a village to make a book. Thanks go out to Storey editors Gwen Steege and Deborah Balmuth, who saw the potential in my draft, and to publisher Pam Art, who believed them and signed me on. Creative director Kent Lew had a vision from the start, and designer Mary Velgos complemented that vision and made it into pages. Thanks to technical editor Lori Gayle for checking the patterns and making sure we got them right, and to Ilona Sherratt and Alison Kolesar for interpreting words into drawings. And many thanks to Elaine Cissi for keeping all these various pieces together.

A very special thank-you goes out to my friend and knitting mentor, Dorothy T. Ratigan. She knows more about knitting than anyone else I know, but throughout this process she made me believe that I know a lot too. In addition to being my technical adviser, Dorothy created the Diamond Classic Cardigan.